Q

TIME WITH THE
PRESIDENT

CW00545148

QUIET
TIME WITH THE
PRESIDENT

PETER FRIEDLAND
with Jill Margo

JONATHAN BALL PUBLISHERS
JOHANNESBURG • CAPE TOWN

All rights reserved.
No part of this publication may be reproduced or transmitted,
in any form or by any means, without prior permission
from the publisher or copyright holder.

© Text: Peter Friedland and Jill Margo (2024)
© Cover image: Gallo Images
© Published edition: Jonathan Ball Publishers (2024)

First published in South Africa in 2024 by
Jonathan Ball Publishers
A division of Media24 (Pty) Ltd
PO Box 33977
Jeppestown
2043

ISBN 978-1-77619-352-3
ebook ISBN 978-1-77619-353-0
audiobook ISBN 978-1-77619-435-3

*Every effort has been made to trace the copyright holders and to obtain their
permission for the use of copyright material. The publishers apologise for any
errors or omissions and would be grateful to be notified of any corrections that
should be incorporated in future editions of this book.*

jonathanball.co.za
x.com/JonathanBallPub
facebook.com/JonathanBallPublishers

Cover by Sean Robertson
Cover image by Win McNamee/Getty Images for the Clinton
    Foundation
Design and typesetting by Martine Barker
Set in Baskerville and New Atten
Printed and bound by Pinetown Printers (Pty) Ltd

— For our parents, Selma and Bernie. —

Contents

Note to the reader

In these pages, I explain how I came to treat Nelson Mandela during the latter years of his life. As demands on him had lessened, he had more time on his hands, and after our medical consultations at his home we would sometimes keep chatting or he would offer me tea. Knowing he wasn't interested in small talk or reminiscing about the past, I made sure I had read the morning newspapers. By the time I got there, he had read them too, so there was always a starting point for a discussion.

Just driving to his house lifted my spirits. I looked forward to seeing that welcoming face and feeling the grace of his presence. It always made me pause and never wore off. To me he was a paradox: a man of steel with a kind of metaphysical power that touched something deep in others, leaving them surprised at feeling so emotional in his presence.

Sometimes I'd be treated to a story or anecdote. He had a particular way of unrolling one and then quietly waiting for me to discern the lesson within it. These parables were often about different aspects of power, and I was hearing them from the master.

I witnessed only fragments of his life, never quite knowing the bigger picture, and never probing too deeply for fear of crossing a line. Just being privy to the thoughts of such an individual seemed gift enough and I didn't want to endanger that honour. But whenever I asked a question, he took the query seriously, answered me thoughtfully and, I felt, with respect.

I've tried to relate these meetings without embellishment. Over the years, there were many stories and I retell some of them here, without the blessing of the authorities who today guard his heritage. I cannot vouch for the veracity of every detail, but I can say that this is what he told me.

As this book was being prepared for publication, so his legacy was being revised in South Africa. The dream he had envisaged when he became president three decades earlier had not been realised and, as the country struggled on, a sense of Mandela fatigue was growing. I believe this is a low point in the cycle of heroism and that in years to come – as the country gets back on its feet – the cycle will turn again. In the larger world, Mandela remains a heroic figure.

I was one of several doctors who treated him in his post-presidential years, and I didn't earn that distinction because of my medical skill. Fate put me in the appropriate place at the right time. That twist of fortune turned out to be the highlight of my professional career and had a profound impact on my personal life.

My experience is framed by undeserved white privilege that delivered great benefits to me. When I started to think independently, it also delivered dilemmas and personal challenges. In this book, I try to explore the powerful forces that push people away from South Africa and then pull them back, until something snaps.

I snapped. I couldn't cope with the violence. Giving my family no option, we held a fire sale and left for Australia on a six-month visa. Mandela had listened silently to my reasons for leaving. Then, after a long pause, he told me of a regrettable mistake he had made in Australia, and gave me a hint of a blessing to go, provided I didn't make the same mistake.

While this text is a piece of 'living history', I have taken great care to maintain the confidentiality of our doctor-patient relationship and divulge nothing of his medical history that is not in the public domain. Volumes have been written about Mandela – by himself, by his family, by people who knew him and by those who didn't. This is a small addition to that legacy.

Peter Friedland

CHAPTER 1

The first phone call

NOTHING MUCH HAPPENS in the South African Army after 3:30 on Friday afternoons. On one such afternoon in February 1991, I had just seen my last patient and was packing up when my desk phone rang. I'd been in the army for almost eight months as a medic and was running an ENT (ear, nose and throat) clinic for military personnel. I picked up. Offering no pleasantries, a male voice barked orders in Afrikaans: 'Present yourself in officer's uniform to the lieutenant colonel at the Witwatersrand High Command at the city barracks in Twist Street at 16:30.'

Before I could ask why or what I'd done wrong, the line was dead. I was a second lieutenant – the most junior rank of officer. That command centre was the largest in the army. To make things worse, my step-outs were at home and not in a presentable state. I looked at my watch. I had 45 minutes.

As I got to the car, I counted myself lucky not to have ducked out a few minutes earlier. Imagine missing such a call! I sped down the highway and, from my new brick of a mobile phone, called home. No answer – oh no. At our house I got dressed as best I could. Back on the highway I called again. My wife answered. 'Linda, I don't know what I've done, but something is terribly wrong and I think I'm going to be court-martialled. Don't expect me for dinner. Tell the guests anything. I may be shot.' She told me to stop babbling and said I was overreacting. But then she didn't understand how the army functioned and what an out-of-the-ordinary command this was.

When I skidded through the gates of the barracks at 4:32 pm, I recognised the officer who was waiting for me. We'd been on a couple of training courses together, but he didn't acknowledge me. He looked me up and down. 'Lieutenant, you're late,' is all he said as he marched me down a corridor towards the large desk behind which the top brass sat. I saluted, stood to attention and braced to hear my fate.

Without looking up, the lieutenant colonel said, in Afrikaans, 'I've received intelligence that tonight there may be an assassination attempt on Mandela.'

Without looking at me or pausing, he began a rapid briefing: 'Mandela and President FW de Klerk will receive a joint media award at 19:00 hours at the Johannesburg Country Club. Each will receive the Johannesburg Press Club's 1990 "Newsmaker of the Year" award; each will make a speech. You will set up medical facilities to manage the assassination attempt.'

The room felt airless. The briefing continued. Two military ambulances and two helicopters would be on site, and

I was to set up two resuscitation stations and coordinate the whole operation. I would have all the staff necessary to get this done.

The plan was that Mandela would walk up first and speak from a lectern at the corner of the stage. A heavy velvet curtain would be drawn across the stage and I was to stand immediately behind the curtain, as close as I could get to him. The intelligence was that he would be shot at the lectern. If and when he returned to his seat, President De Klerk would then come up and I was to remain in position. I would be given a civilian suit to wear.

By now I was wiggling my toes – an old parade-ground trick to avoid passing out. When the briefing finished, I nervously raised an issue.

'Colonel, if I stand behind Mr Mandela and he gets shot, I'll likely take a bullet too and there won't be anyone to—'

For the first time he glanced up, and, with a sneer, cut me off. 'Orders are orders. Dismissed.'

From the army stores, where 'one size fits no one', I was handed a dark blue suit, a white shirt and a tie. I found a moment to call Linda to say I had to attend a function but couldn't disclose the details. I definitely wouldn't be home for the Sabbath meal. She asked why I had been chosen. I had no idea. Perhaps it was because my clinic at the JG Strijdom Hospital was two kilometres from the country club. But then this hospital, named after a former apartheid prime minister, was not yet admitting people of colour. But helicopters would be there to take the injured to 1 Mil in Pretoria, the biggest military hospital in Africa. Things were happening so fast I couldn't think beyond the immediate logistics.

We got the equipment to the venue and were fully set up by 6:30 pm, leaving me time to scout the club complex that I'd heard so much about. The old hall could seat a few hundred and was already filling up. I recognised a couple of local white celebrities, captains of industry and some journalists. Someone said this was the first time Mandela and De Klerk would be appearing on a joint public platform, acknowledging each other's work in the push to end apartheid.

At the time, these two men had different views about how the post-apartheid system might look and there was tension between them. They were working towards a new constitution for the country, and both had to contend with furious opposition within their own ranks. To appease his angry constituents, De Klerk, who had been president of South Africa since 1989, wanted whites to have some form of veto or other special rights in the new constitution. Mandela, who had been out of jail for just a year, rejected this outright. There would be no compromise on a one-person-one-vote system. There would be a majority government.

I was two years old when Mandela went to jail and grew up never hearing his voice or knowing what he looked like. It was the height of apartheid and the South African government had demonised him to such an extent that it was a crime to utter his name. On the rare occasion that I did hear it, it had a mythical ring. All I really knew was that he was a major figure in the fight against apartheid.

Later I learned that on 9 October 1963, the day I turned

two, he was in the dock at the Palace of Justice in Pretoria, charged with sabotage, promotion of guerrilla warfare and planning an armed invasion. At the age of 45, he was about to put his stamp on one of the most consequential political trials of the century. He had come to believe that controlled violence was the only way to effect change in South Africa and was commander-in-chief of the African National Congress's armed wing, Umkhonto we Sizwe (Spear of the Nation). As the oldest liberation movement in Africa, the ANC had spent 50 years peacefully propagating its cause, without significant success. In 1960 it was banned, and the following year it shifted from nonviolent to violent means of opposing apartheid.

The next three years were intense for Mandela. In 1961, together with many other defendants, he was finally acquitted following a treason trial that had dragged on for more than five years. Immediately, he went underground, and in 1962 travelled widely in Africa and visited London organising support for the ANC and undergoing military training. But, later that year, he was arrested and charged with incitement and leaving South Africa illegally. Before he could serve the five-year sentence for these two 'crimes' he was back in the dock, in October 1963.

Mandela did not bother disputing the new charges. A lawyer by training, he conducted his own defence and turned the trial on its head. In front of an international audience, he put the government on trial for the injustice of apartheid. He took full responsibility for his actions and, with no fear, said he was prepared to die for his ideals. His courage and dignity touched something universal and people couldn't look away.

There was no question that the judge would find him guilty as charged. The only question was what his punishment would be. The state wanted the death penalty but bowed to international pressure and sentenced him to life in prison. But it also slapped on a banning order of biblical proportions, making it illegal for anyone to mention Mandela's name, display his image, write about him, or use any words that had been spoken or written by him.

The intention was to blot him out until he faded from memory. But instead, by suppressing all information about him, the state created a vacuum in which the legend of Mandela grew. This invisible man became a mighty force-in-waiting, a force expected to liberate millions.

And there was more. He and his co-accused were incarcerated on Robben Island, and over the years, as younger black activists were sentenced and arrived on the island, so they were mentored by the older men, led by Mandela. While Robben Island may have been a desolate windswept prison just off Cape Town, it was also an incubator.

The most stunning contradiction is how confinement can set the mind free, and how Mandela possibly became the best modern example of this. After an intensely frenetic life, jail gave him long stretches of contemplative time alone in his tiny cell. All that energy that he once put out was turned inward. He used those long years to think beyond conventional boundaries and to make internal adjustments that would shape him into the statesman he became.

These adjustments would change his approach to politics, which in turn would enable a peaceful transition to majority rule. While this came at immeasurable personal cost to Mandela and his loved ones, it saved the country from a blood-soaked revolution.

In South Africa, a life sentence was usually 21 years, but for him it would be 27. During those years, more than a hundred awards and honours were bestowed upon him outside South Africa. Around the world, streets, squares and parks were named after him. So was a nuclear particle. There were prizes in his name, medals were struck and honorary academic positions conferred. There was no internet then, and as none of this could be reported by the traditional media inside the country, I knew nothing of it.

One of his biographers tells how once, after a medical check-up in Cape Town, Mandela's jailers allowed him a brief walk on a public beach. As expected, he passed unnoticed. I first glimpsed a photograph of him at Baragwanath Hospital in Soweto in the 1980s, when a young black doctor momentarily opened his locker next to mine. The photo was taped to the inside of the door, and it dated from the time of his trial.

CHAPTER 2

Behind the velvet curtain

F ROM NOWHERE, Mandela suddenly materialised in our lives. The negotiations behind the scenes had been kept from the poorly informed public, and he re-entered our lives through two distinct events, nine days apart, in February 1990.

Back then, I was a trainee in ear, nose and throat surgery at the once grand Johannesburg General Hospital (now the Charlotte Maxeke Johannesburg Academic Hospital). This sprawling Victorian estate, with large airy wards that would have pleased Florence Nightingale, had once been for the exclusive use of white people. When a modern, First-World hospital was opened on nearby Parktown Ridge, they moved there. As a student in the mid-1980s, I witnessed this old hospital briefly closing and, despite loud protests, much of its best equipment being relocated to Parktown Ridge. Then, without restocking, this old site was renamed Hillbrow Hospital and reopened for black people.

Although it had fallen into disrepair, the bones of the buildings were beautiful, with their arches, passageways and lightwells. Glass viewing platforms where students could watch operations were also still in place. I watched many, but more interesting to me was how this hospital reflected racial politics. It dated back a century and initially it had treated everyone, regardless of race. In 1924 this changed, and for the next sixty years or so it only served whites. Now, in a poorer condition, it only served blacks.

On Friday morning, 2 February, I was in one of its large wards performing a bedside surgical procedure on a patient who was lying very still. My headlight was on and I was concentrating intensely when a sudden commotion disturbed us both. Staff and patients who could walk were moving down the aisle to the far end of the ward, where a small television set was perched high on the wall. President FW de Klerk was addressing the nation.

At the time, South Africa was in a state of emergency. Large-scale rioting was a daily occurrence, there was blood on the streets and the country was braced for more violence. But rather than announcing a few mild, conciliatory reforms, as was expected, the president was departing from his party line. Patients in starched white gowns holding their drip stands, nurses, doctors, porters and cleaners all stood together, looking up, mouths open.

De Klerk was unbanning every single banned organisation in the country, from the ANC to the Communist Party. He was repealing apartheid laws and all the institutionalised racism they enforced, from forbidden marriages between races to restrictions on where people could live. We were stunned.

Then came the grenade. With immediate effect, he would release all political prisoners, including the biggest antihero of them all, Nelson Mandela. With this, the small crowd burst apart. There was dancing and ululating through the ward as patients clapped and cheered from their antique beds. Over the last years, the ruling party had slowly been loosening the scaffolding of apartheid, but this would be its demolition. For the people in the ward and for most of the nation, that day opened a future of hope and freedom.

For many white people, however, the heavens fell. They expected Mandela would be released the next day and, together with other newly freed political prisoners, would waste no time taking revenge for the brutality of apartheid. But Mandela didn't want to leave the timing of his freedom in the hands of his oppressors. He wanted to make his own arrangements with his family and the ANC before he walked free.

In 1984, he had declined an offer for a conditional release that would see him confined to a remote 'homeland' in South Africa. Again, in 1985, he declined another offer conditional on the renunciation of violence. He would not accept freedom in a country that was not free. But this time, with De Klerk in charge, it would be different. Without the knowledge of the ANC, Mandela had acted alone and in 1989 had conducted secret discussions with De Klerk.

In his memoir, *The Last Trek: A New Beginning*, De Klerk describes how Mandela was smuggled into the Cape Town presidential office complex, Tuynhuys, via the basement garage. This was their first meeting and, for most of it, each 'cautiously sized up the other'. To De Klerk, Mandela was dignified, courteous and confident, with an ability 'to radiate unusual warmth and charm – when he so chose'. Despite this qualifier, Mandela's standing was so high that De Klerk trusted him enough to put his own future at risk and negotiate with him.

De Klerk insisted that he alone would remain in control of the timing of Mandela's release. The world would be watching, and while Mandela could not choose the date, he would be permitted to choose the place and time of day. Although he knew apartheid had to end, and end quickly, De Klerk had been profoundly courageous to close the book on apartheid so suddenly. There was no doubt that he would face rebellion from extreme elements in his own party. But world opinion and economic pressure had already forced some changes, and within the Afrikaner community, the quest to establish a religious basis for apartheid had been abandoned.

De Klerk's speech set off seismic waves of both fear and elation across the country. Was it possible that a transition to majority rule could take place peacefully? No one knew. Over the next days, there were ominous reports of whites stockpiling food and buying guns.

Time magazine rushed to put Mandela on the cover of its 5 February 1990 edition. But, like the rest of the world, it didn't have a contemporary photograph. In 1964, a reporter from *The Daily Telegraph* in London had taken some shots of Mandela as a prisoner on Robben Island. In 1977, there was an international press junket to Robben Island and a rather attractive photo of 'a prisoner in the garden', well dressed and wearing a hat and sunglasses, was handed out. One journalist looked at the face and realised it was Mandela. It was reported that the warder then scratched out the face.

While all these photos were banned in South Africa, they were available to the rest of the world, and it is likely *Time* built its cover image from them. The result, unsurprisingly, bore no resemblance to the man who emerged from prison nine days after De Klerk's announcement.

When De Klerk made that announcement, I never imagined I would meet Mandela. Why would I? I was an unknown junior doctor, barely out of medical school. He was one of the most famous incarcerated political leaders of modern times and was about to emerge onto the world stage. There seemed no way our paths would cross.

But exactly a year later, I would be standing centimetres behind him, entrusted with saving his life (and afraid of losing my own). I was only there because I had deferred my compulsory army service. At 17, when most of the boys in my class were conscripted following school, I was able to defer by studying veterinary science. After four years of that, I switched to medicine and was permitted to defer again.

When I finally graduated, no one came for me, and I hoped I had been forgotten. But in January 1990 the military police caught up with me. They knocked on my door with an ultimatum: complete compulsory service for 12 months or go to prison for two years as a conscientious objector.

With my son Gavriel just two years old and Linda pregnant with twins, I agreed to join up that July. I didn't know that I would be part of the last mandatory conscription for national service. After Mandela was released, the conscription was abandoned. At least, after my basics and officer training, I was stationed at a hospital not too far from home.

Alone on the semi-darkened stage, I looked around, trying to imagine where an assassin might be hiding. There were plenty of places in the wings, but then I looked up. The lighting grids and footholds offered good vantage points too. There seemed to be no security police around, although they might have been out of sight and in plain clothes. It occurred to me that this exclusive country club, which had upheld solid colonial views for almost a century, didn't admit black, Asian, Indian or Jewish people. Now it was hosting a revered black freedom fighter and a junior Jewish doctor.

It had been a year since Mandela's release and the country was still deeply unsettled, with open talk of civil war. After more than three centuries of white domination, the extremist right was not going to relinquish its entitlements without a fight. It was smarting from the whiplash of the change and the swift unlocking of a prison gate so Nelson Mandela could walk free on a summer afternoon.

With nothing more to do except wait for gunfire, I started to replay the afternoon of his release in my mind. The world had been waiting for this historic event, and Linda and I had planned to watch it at home, undisturbed. But I was doing an after-hours 'on call locum' at the nearby nursing home where my late father had been a patient. Half an hour before the big moment, I was called out. A patient needed my help. I resigned myself to watching a replay on the news that night and drove to the nursing home.

When the consultation was over, both the patient and I were thrilled to hear that Mandela's release had been delayed. So I pushed his wheelchair to the lounge where other residents were gathered around a television. As I couldn't risk trying to get home, I settled in with the residents.

Anticipation was high. Mandela hadn't been sighted since 1964 and, given that he had spent much of his sentence on Robben Island, no one knew what to expect.

Eventually a tall, greying man walked slowly into view. Holding his wife's hand, he looked a little tentative and gave a half-wave. Then, gaining confidence, he raised both arms in a salute, smiled warmly and moved through the enthusiastic crowd that had broken through the police cordon. People wanted to touch him.

The residents in the lounge were surprised. He looked nothing like the devil incarnate who, for their safety, had been forcibly silenced. His face was open and appealing. He greeted people and shook their hands. He wasn't an evil force, and he wasn't a broken man. Rather, he cut an elegant, dignified figure, fully in command of himself.

This monumental event unfolded on a country road on an otherwise ordinary Sunday afternoon. Despite its international importance, it appeared totally unchoreographed. Mandela wasn't walking down a flag-lined boulevard, there was no balcony and there were no fanfare trumpets. Years later, it would be revealed that while he chose the location, the authorities deliberately designed the process to be as undramatic as possible. They said it was for security reasons. Who knows?

Along the way, people kept surrounding his car as it slowly moved towards the heart of Cape Town, where more than a quarter of a million people had been waiting in the sun for hours. I saw an opportunity and dashed home, to continue watching with Linda. Actually, I needn't have rushed. Mandela's trip took far longer than expected and by the time he arrived at the City Hall, there was mayhem. Rioting had broken out on the periphery of the crowd before his arrival and the police had opened fire.

Despite this, Mandela insisted on attending the gathering. This time there was a balcony, and from it he spoke to the waiting nation. The crowd hushed, hanging on to every word. He promised there would be freedom and rights for all, a place for everybody and no revenge.

At that moment, I realised the little I'd heard about him from official sources had been distorted. There seemed to be no rage or rancour in him, and I was riveted. Later I would learn that, quite naturally, he had feelings of bitterness and anger but that his greatness lay in his ability to control them. Externally at least, Mandela appeared calm.

But now, behind the curtain, waiting for Mandela to fall backwards into my arms, I could not calm myself. With 20 minutes to kill, I decided to go outside for some air and to check on my medical teams. Everyone else seemed agitated too. There was a big army presence behind the building and these uniformed men were restless. What was going on? I hung around and as I listened to their conversation in Afrikaans, I realised they were furious at De Klerk for throwing away their heritage.

These were right-wing Permanent Force (the term used for South Africa's standing army at that time) Afrikaners who had defended South Africa against communism and hostile border incursions, and who for decades had fought the 'Swart Gevaar', the 'Black Danger'. Now, they were being asked to protect the man who was putting them in danger. The numbers were against them, and they feared a potential bloodbath, with 30 million blacks putting the country's 5 million whites to death.

These career soldiers had been brought up, taught in the schoolroom and long encouraged from the pulpit to believe their mission was to bring enlightenment to the indigenous population. Their church held that whites were the fruits of Christian civilisation and gave them the right to rule and to limit the human rights of the colonised population. Now, look what was happening. As I listened, it occurred to me for the first time that perhaps I might also have to resuscitate De Klerk. That would explain the duplication of resuscitation facilities.

My thoughts were interrupted by the arrival of Mandela's motorcade. As it rolled in, the soldiers were even more put out. He was in a classic, new red Mercedes-Benz 500 SE. This car symbolised so much. Hundreds of workers in the Mercedes factory in East London had banded together to build it for him. A day after his release from prison, they persuaded the factory's management to supply the components and then they systematically assembled the vehicle in their own time, free of charge.

It was a project of pure passion. As Phillip Groom, who was instrumental in the project, told *CarMag*, 'From the moment the car was merely a skeleton, and every time it was passed onto the next station, the workers would gather around the car, like in a ceremony, dancing as it passed them.' In those days there was a long waiting list for expensive German cars and the standard joke was that Mandela had been on the waiting list for 27 years.

The soldiers, of course, didn't approve of the car and were further affronted that he had arrived with his own security detail. These black men were armed with guns and semi-automatic rifles. The cheek of it!

Minutes later, De Klerk arrived with his well-armed white security detail, which the soldiers felt was appropriate and which they begrudgingly respected. At that point I returned to my post.

CHAPTER 3

Where did the bitterness go?

I WAS IN TIME to see the two men walk into the hall together, to a standing ovation. Peeping through the curtain, I could feel shivers down my spine. The power of two old adversaries coming down the aisle, side by side, was something to behold. I'd seen De Klerk live before, but this was my first glimpse of Mandela in the flesh. He was almost majestic. De Klerk was a big man, but Mandela towered over him. The symbolism was clear, and when they sat in the front row, the house sat too.

Mandela had the bearing of a member of the royal family of the isiXhosa-speaking Thembu tribe. He was a young boy when his father, a principal counsellor to the acting king of the Thembu people, died. The regent stepped in and took care of the boy. I'd read something of his ancestry and, out of respect, when others addressed Mandela by his clan name of Madiba, I decided I would do the same if ever I got the opportunity to speak to him.

As the evening progressed, I grew more anxious. When Madiba came up on stage, I stood centimetres behind him and thought I could feel the heat off his body. Waiting for the first bullet, I didn't absorb a word of his speech. I was overthinking the situation. Perhaps this was deliberately planned by the army. If Madiba was going to be shot, so was I, and there would be no one medically qualified to resuscitate him. More likely the army hadn't thought it through.

Mandela finished his speech and, to rapturous applause, returned to his seat. Nothing had happened. Then I thought, 'Oh my God, now they're going to shoot De Klerk.' He wouldn't be the first Afrikaner leader to be taken out. I searched my memory for the story about a deranged white farmer shooting Dr Hendrik Verwoerd, the chief architect of apartheid. As prime minister, he was shot twice in the head at an Easter cattle show in Johannesburg.

Suddenly, it came to me. I remembered Linda's father, Dr Israel (Boomie) Abramowitz, telling me the story of how he had resuscitated Verwoerd. As a newly qualified vascular surgeon, he was on duty at the old Johannesburg General Hospital when Verwoerd was rushed into the emergency department. Boomie worked on him, stabilised him, and then transferred him to the old 1 Mil Hospital in Pretoria. That was in 1960 and he survived. Six years later, a second attempt was successful when a uniformed messenger, Dmitri Tsafendas, stabbed him in parliament.

The potential parallel with my father-in-law unnerved me even more. An assassination attempt on De Klerk would be on almost the same ground as the Verwoerd shooting. Back in those days, the cattle show was held very close to this country club. My mind was running away from me but returned abruptly when I heard De Klerk's footsteps on the stairs. As he stood at the podium, I felt his presence just as I had felt Madiba's.

Although I was listening acutely, it was not to his speech. I was trying to catch any sound out of the ordinary. But, despite myself, I heard him referring to a measure of resistance to change, saying, 'Many of our people, quite understandably, are uncertain and fearful about the future.' This chimed with the sentiment among the soldiers outside the hall and gave me no comfort. Then his speech was over. There was clapping. Again, nothing bad had happened. My new suit was drenched.

Once the hall had emptied, we packed up and I was given a lift home in one of the military ambulances. The corporal at the wheel was spitting mad and insulting De Klerk in the vulgar manner in which army corporals excel. He lamented that De Klerk had not been blown to pieces and repeated how he would like to have killed him with his own two hands. He was incensed that he had to be there on a Friday night, and asked why the hell I was there. Why would I want to aid De Klerk or Mandela if they needed resuscitation?

He was driving like a lunatic, at about 160 kilometres an hour down the M1, and I felt he was going to kill me. He wanted my address, but he was so vicious that I didn't trust him and insisted he drop me at the Corlett Drive off-ramp, saying I lived right next to it. He wouldn't hear of it, and when I persisted, he screeched to a halt and ordered me out and onto the motorway. It was near enough to my ramp, so I got out and, with trembling legs, walked the rest of the way home. The Friday-night candles were still burning in the sleeping household. On an empty stomach, I downed a double Johnnie Walker.

Neither the next day, nor ever, did anyone from the army follow up on the event. It simply dropped away, as if it had never happened. But from then on, I followed the unfolding political scene with fresh interest, never imagining I'd ever come close to Madiba again.

At 71, his urgent mission was to see the majority enfranchised, and he let it be known clearly that his agenda was not against white supremacy; it was against all supremacy. But the more goodwill he expressed, the more fearful the white right became.

Soon there were whispers of a 'third force' fomenting violence and fuelling the unrest. Clandestine groups of police, Defence Force personnel, mercenaries, the black political organisation Inkatha and right-wing agitators, supported by elements in government, began killing hundreds of people, blowing up ANC meetings and doing their best to disrupt the impending change.

Whenever Madiba appeared on television I'd stop to watch, hoping for a clue to what lay behind that enlightened face. It would be almost a decade before he became my patient, by which time I'd been through the troubles of those intervening years. In the streets of Johannesburg, in my own home and in the hospital's trauma unit, I experienced the full force of the violence that plagued the country. From crouching behind bushes with my two young sons, inches away from an unfolding hijacking, to holding the body of a good friend as he bled out, to working deep in a neck shattered by bullets, it was terrifying. The smell of fear, blood and body fluids in the trauma unit still comes back to me.

But so does something else from those difficult days. In extraordinary moments, trauma surgery can take you beyond your limits. This does not happen often, but you find yourself working on the edge of survival, in a zone where the difference between you and the patient almost falls away. To the naked eye, all your professional training has come to the fore and you are operating silently, with surgical precision. In yourself, however, you have descended into some deep pre-conscious territory and are using the full force of your being to hold on to another being that is in dire danger. Such moments are rare, indelible and universal.

I'm almost reluctant to describe those moments, but they gave me a glimpse of the territory where much of Madiba's 'magic', as it came to be known, had its effect. When people felt this, it wasn't because he was speaking to their heads or to their hearts. They felt it before he had uttered a word. I think it was because he was reaching beyond individuality, to the deep source of humankind, and they felt the commonality.

One of the less discussed things about Madiba was that, after almost three decades of confinement, he was expected to step into the open and, without blinking, take charge. Some might say he'd had a long time to prepare, but he'd also been institutionalised, and I knew what that meant. I'd seen how some of my older patients lost their sense of independence after only two or three weeks in hospital.

Their confidence was diminished and they worried that they wouldn't cope alone at home.

Released from long sentences, prisoners often have difficulty adapting to life outside. Rigid routines of jail, imprinted over many long years, don't easily disappear, and personal habits that gave them comfort in their cells can be hard to give up. Madiba was used to spending contemplative hours alone but, by all accounts, after his release there was no time for that kind of open-ended free thinking. In its place there was an abundance of recognition, with people clamouring for his attention and much work to do.

From several books about his life, we know that he was left with no time to gather his loved ones and slowly repair frayed family ties. He was thrust directly into the role of rescuing the country. His job was to make it a fair, safe place for everyone. This had not been done in modern South Africa before, there was no template to follow and the responsibility was enormous. He had a dream, but he didn't have very much time left to make it an enduring reality. Others would have to do that.

He was also re-entering a world that had changed in so many ways. Years later, he told me he'd been struck by the number of cars on the road and how different they looked. He particularly noticed how many more black people were driving and remarked on the number of women too. Since boyhood, when he was entrusted to the Thembu regent, cars had been an important symbol for him. He'd never forgotten the regent's large American car, often driven by a chauffeur. In his young world, it was one of a kind.

When he was last free, he had driven a flashy two-tone Oldsmobile through the dusty streets of Soweto to his law practice in the city. The car had been a local sensation and everyone in that township had recognised it and him. Back then, it was a big deal for a black man to own a car. Now people of all colours were speeding down multi-lane highways, and the world was being described as a global village.

While the ANC had had no real opportunity to prepare to take the levers of national government, Madiba was even less prepared. Having been locked away for so long, he wasn't worldly and he knew it. Once, when he had already been my patient for some years, he mentioned that he hadn't felt equipped to be president. There was so much he had missed and there was too much he didn't know. How could he walk onto the world stage and engage with current events, as if he'd lived through them and understood their context? To illustrate this, he told me about an episode in Australia that had exposed his ignorance and left him acutely embarrassed. More about that later.

On his release he was, however, ready to roll up his sleeves and start working with De Klerk to transform South Africa into a democracy. This behind-the-scenes work had to be done before the next election, and the transition was tricky for both of them. Their negotiation process dominated the news, with the two men repeatedly having confrontations – some nasty – and then resolving them.

In 1993, they were photographed together at the World Economic Forum in Davos, and then in Sweden, where they were jointly awarded the Nobel Peace Prize for their work in ending apartheid. Years later, De Klerk disclosed that Madiba had done something unexpected on that trip. The day after the award ceremony, they went to a banquet in Oslo where Madiba made a surprisingly personal speech, allowing some of his 'understandable bitterness' to come out. This was so rare it was noteworthy. De Klerk heard that Madiba had not been pleased with the decision to share the prize.

That aside, everyone was curious about his general lack of bitterness. It underpinned his moral stature and people wondered where it had come from. A great part of it seemed to come from those long hours alone during which he remade himself. The solitude of that prison cell enabled him to take a step that most of us would find counter-intuitive. It was recognising the humanity of the oppressor. Without losing sight of what had happened, he was able to descend past the actions, to the source. One commentator said Madiba saw that the oppressed and the oppressor were in a bind and that release from it had to be a mutual process. Each had to release the other, and to achieve this, there had to be recognition of what had happened, and forgiveness.

Forgiveness was a strategy for survival, and Madiba lived it so that it almost became part of him. Later, he would write that as he walked out of prison, he knew that if he didn't leave his bitterness and hatred behind, he would still be imprisoned. Many years later, US President Bill Clinton reported a snippet of conversation that touched on this. He asked Madiba how he had really felt the day he walked free. 'Tell me the truth. Weren't you really angry all over again?' Madiba replied that he had been angry and a little afraid, 'but when I felt that anger well up inside me, I realised that if I hated them after I got outside, they still had me. I wanted to be free, so I let it go in my life. It changed me.' Clinton commented that while Madiba did have flashes of regret and anger, in the big moments there was no one like him.

In the lead-up to the election, Madiba privately argued that he was too old and not contemporary enough to lead the country. But the pressure was immense, the enthusiasm was irresistible, and in 1994 he was inaugurated as president of the national unity government of South Africa. As the oldest head of state in the country's history, he agreed to a single term of office. He would serve his five years and not seek re-election at the age of 81.

De Klerk, who became his deputy, admitted that bad things had been done in the name of apartheid, and apologised more than once, but most people felt this wasn't sincere. Personally, I was tremendously optimistic about our new rainbow nation and was thrilled that Linda and I had stayed in South Africa to witness its emergence. So many people close to us had left, including my two sisters, Linda's sister and several of our relatives.

I was in my early thirties, weeks away from qualifying as an ear, nose and throat surgeon, and while there had been times when I wanted to run, now nothing could drag me away.

CHAPTER 4

A dim awareness

WHILE I WAS GROWING UP, apartheid was present in all aspects of South African life and the only way to escape it completely was to leave. This was not an option for my family. We stayed and voted against the ruling party but took no real risks. To alleviate suffering, we did small, good deeds in our immediate surroundings, spoke out and worked on election campaigns for the opposition, but all within the system from which we benefited because of the colour of our skin.

By way of explanation, not excuse, we had our difficulties. Before I began school, my father, Bernie, was struck with a rapidly progressive neurological disease and, over the next six years, although he found work, he could cope with less and less and eventually couldn't manage any at all.

Towards the end of the day, I'd sit in a syringa tree that gave me a clear view of the intersection at the top of our street. I couldn't see as far as the bus stop, but as soon as my father turned the corner, I'd jump down, run up the small hill and take his arm to steady him. Looking through their windows, the neighbours probably assumed he was drunk, again. All the other fathers in the street were healthy and to see his wide, unsteady gait pained me deeply. My brother and I would assist him on the toilet, in the shower and with dressing, but in that phase of his illness he was angry and frustrated. He needed our help but didn't want our sympathy and we were left confused.

My mother, Selma, was a schoolteacher and from then on, she never had fewer than two jobs. There were four children – Sally, Jill, my identical twin Richard and me – as well as my father and the household to maintain. At no point did she allow us to feel sorry for ourselves. Rather, she'd remind us that it was a blessing that we were healthy enough to help our father. She was showing us another realm which, in retrospect, we only partially grasped. But being so young and having so little information, we didn't know what the future held. The magical thinking of childhood allowed us to imagine him getting better, the way other adults got better, driving us to school and teaching us to play rugby, a sport he'd once played well and loved.

At fixed times of the school calendar, Richard and I would get up at sunrise to help our mother mark state exam papers stacked in neat bundles beside our dining table. A modest sum could be earned per paper, and while she marked the history essays, we'd do the multiple choice, proof each other's work, add the marks and recheck the totals. Then we'd go to school.

As we got older, all four children had bits of work

outside the house, and we handed all earnings directly to our mother. Our father was a civil engineer who loved his job, and I clearly remember the Friday of his devastating final retrenchment. My mother was beside herself, so Richard and I went out looking for real work.

Eventually we landed at Kaufie's Bakery, famed for its bagels. A greying Mr Kaufman took one look at us and asked us how old we were. The legal age for employment was 16. Not only were we 11 but we were short for our age. So we said 14. He looked at us as if he understood our whole history and said, 'Boys, I'll give you a job, 7 am to 7 pm on Sundays, 45 cents an hour, no lunch.' Then, at the door, he called us back. 'I know you boys won't steal from me.' We looked at him. 'Because you are such poor liars.' For the next couple of years, we stood on crates to see over the high glass counters.

Whenever we complained about not having the things our friends had, our mother swiftly readjusted our perspective. 'Children in Alexandra [the township near our home] have far less than you. They'd be grateful for what you have,' she would say. That was her standard response and we learned that moaning was pointless.

We'd waited a very long time to get our first bicycles and one afternoon, a couple of black kids watched us riding up and down our street. 'Can I have a chance?' one asked. I declined. 'You only say that because I'm black,' he said. So I offered him a ride and he immediately rode away. By the time we realised what had happened − and Richard went after him − it was too late. My mother wiped away my angry tears but noted the bike would probably mean much more to that young boy. It made me furious. A couple of weeks later, Richard's bike was stolen from outside our front door, and that was that.

Although the hat was passed around our extended family, towards the end of each month things were often thin, and Mr Green from the local Spar supermarket would give us groceries on credit. Still, compared to the overwhelming majority of South Africans we remained highly advantaged, with access to opportunities unavailable to them.

The notion of equal opportunity did not exist in South Africa. White people sat atop the pyramid with full entitlement. People from Asia, India and those of mixed race filled the middle, and black people were at the base with minimal entitlement. The stratification was clear-cut and inhumane.

In my relatively sheltered suburban existence, disparities were all around me, but I was only dimly aware of what lay behind them. It would take me years to make sense of what was really going on. I remember how, late on Saturday nights, black boys of 10 or 11 would be selling the Sunday papers at traffic lights. As they weaved between the cars, posting their wares through the windows, they hoped for a tiny tip in return. In mid-winter and in rain, these boys were often barefoot. How they got home – wherever home was – was not much of a concern for those who drove on. For most whites, there was no social responsibility across the colour bar, and no obligation to act.

What did my family do at those traffic lights? Not much. We'd pass a little extra cash through the window, and if we happened to have a cardigan or something warm in the car, we'd pass it too. Those boys were symptomatic of a vast cancer that had taken hold of the country. Like the disease, you couldn't quite see it, but you could see its consequences.

All we could offer were small plasters, mostly ineffective but occasionally worthwhile.

In those days, having full-time domestic help was the norm in many white homes. We called these people maids or servants, and they lived in small, cramped outbuildings in the rear of each house. They'd left their own homes and families to look after ours. I was born into this and would spend time in the backyard with Dora Masemola, sitting on the concrete floor of her room, eating the spinach (morogo) she cooked on a small paraffin stove. Sometimes I'd hang around Jacob Ramoroka, a kind and thoughtful adult man we referred to as 'the garden boy'. Those were the days when my father could still work.

Jacob's dexterity and intelligence impressed my father and together they devised an alternate career for him. Sponsored by my parents, Jacob became one of the first black people to enroll in a Swiss watchmaking and repair course. He continued to live with us and did so well in his course that he was sent to further his skills in Switzerland. On his return, he took a modest room in the city, put up a sign and became one of the first black Swiss watch repairers in Johannesburg. I remember visiting him there, but not fully understanding my father's excitement or Jacob's achievement.

At high school the fog began to lift and I began to see just a little more clearly. This was a slow awakening, and in my penultimate year I started to do small-scale things. As a bursary student to King David High School, I was expected to behave well, shut up and be grateful. And I was grateful, but I couldn't keep quiet. I managed to organise a peaceful protest about people suffering in a squatter camp, but the posters I put around the school were removed immediately. Then I hit on the idea of inviting speakers to come to assembly to educate us about the horrors of apartheid. For the headmaster, Mr Elliot Wolf, inviting left-wingers in the 1970s was a 'no-no' as it might compromise this private school's government subsidies. He urged me to desist.

I didn't. Percy Qoboza, who had been editor-in-chief of *The World*, a newspaper for black readers, accepted the invitation. So did Ernie Wentzel, an outstanding lawyer who defended many in the struggle for equal rights. Hans Strydom, co-author of the brave and explosive book *The Super-Afrikaners*, which exposed the secret workings of a powerful and secret Afrikaner organisation called the Broederbond, came too. Even scandal-ridden Dr Connie Mulder, who was once tipped to become prime minister, spoke to us. I don't know what this achieved, but it stirred something in me that would not be quietened when I went to university the following year.

My brother and I enrolled at the University of Pretoria, the only institution in the country that offered a veterinary degree. Our choice was largely shaped by what had happened to our father. Others can, but I can't remember him as the once strong, warm centre of our family. Others say he was fit and optimistic before his neurological disease slowly destroyed him. In those days diagnostic tools were not well developed and doctors struggled to make a diagnosis. One declared he had 'nervous tension, burning itself out' – a common description for what has since become known as PTSD.

He'd been blown up in a jeep in combat in the 1940s and the doctor tied his condition to that. But this made no sense to my father, and his ongoing search to try to understand what was really happening was heartbreaking.

This was the era of psychosomatic medicine and the pendulum had swung too far. Exasperated and desperate, he appeared before a panel of specialists at a mental institution that confirmed he had a psychosomatic disorder. These esteemed experts used fancy language but what they meant was that he wasn't physically ill; he just thought he was. His failing vision was attributed to hysterical blindness. His increasing clumsiness was a product of his disturbed mind. Although he could no longer shave himself and was too weak to get up from a fall, it was implied that if he could only get his mind in order, he'd be able to walk, get back to productive work and support his family. There was so much agony in this misdiagnosis.

Psychosomatic medicine was supposed to bring a deeper understanding to illness and assist in healing. But in his case, it was only harmful. As medical technology became more sophisticated, my father was found to have demyelinating disease, a condition that damages the protective covering around nerves. Finally, a CT scan confirmed incurable advanced multiple sclerosis. He would never get better, just progressively worse.

Witnessing what was happening to our humble parents made Richard and me angry. We didn't understand the complexities, and, with youthful outrage, we wrote off the entire medical profession. Several of our friends were talking about doing medicine at university, but we didn't even consider it. Anyway, our mother said there were enough doctors in the world and suggested we turn to animals and help them. So we borrowed all the Gerald Durrell and James Herriot books from our local library, volunteered at veterinary clinics and became committed vets-in-waiting. We focused on being accepted into veterinary school and, as the majority of our courses would be in Afrikaans, we began reading the Afrikaans newspapers every day.

Veterinary science was the most expensive undergraduate course in the country, with fees, travel and lodgings beyond our reach. With the help of my father's older brother, Meyer, who was an electrician, we spent part of our weekends at the dining room table, handwriting letters to countless organisations that were offering bursaries and funding. Ashamed of our neediness, we kept this a secret from our classmates and extended family. A few days a week after school we worked as cashiers at the local supermarket until closing at 8:30 pm.

After examining all our earnings and our budget, the Jewish Women's Benevolent Society agreed to give us R30 a month. That was a relief. Then, the day after our final school exams, we started eight weeks of work. Richard took a job in a hardware yard, and I went to an accounting firm. As the Faculty of Veterinary Science was at Onderstepoort, north of Pretoria, we would need a car. Our joint holiday earnings paid for a ten-year-old VW Beetle, and I can tell you it never had a full tank. We would put in the minimum amount of fuel and then freewheel down the highway, seeing how far we could push it, and enjoying the uncertainty of making it home. Then, we agreed to have our VW repainted so that it was almost entirely covered in fruit, to advertise the popular drink, Liqui Fruit. This attracted a lot of attention and people were doubly surprised when identical twins climbed out and distributed samples.

The vet school was simply known as 'Onderstepoort', and while it had earned international acclaim for developing several animal vaccines, it also had a reputation for being a bastion of extreme right-wing opinion. The quota for Jewish students in our year was four. It was the first year black students were admitted and their quota was two.

At the beginning of the academic year, first-year students from all faculties had to attend an introductory lecture at the University of Pretoria. I sat with my class, in front of a full-sized ox-wagon housed in glass. The wagon was a powerful symbol of Afrikaner nationalism: it represented the Great Trek, which saw more than 12 000 Boers leave the Cape Colony and push into the 'unknown' north. In wagon trains, these Dutch-speaking immigrants were escaping the British and hoping to find freedom and fresh farmland.

Almost a century and a half later, this wagon evoked mixed feelings in our class. It made the Afrikaner students proud of their pioneering heritage, of the vision and fortitude of their ancestors. For black students, the wagon symbolised invasion, war, loss and oppression. For me it was different. My family was relatively new to the country. They'd come early in the century to escape persecution in Europe and had found safety. As a second-generation South African, I felt attached to the country of my birth and, by then, was well aware of how much better a place it could become.

That introductory lecture included a homily on the God-given foundation of Afrikaner ideology and apartheid. It was delivered in Afrikaans, and we were told campus life would be guided by conservative ethics and principles of the Afrikaans Nederduitse Gereformeerde Kerk (NGK, a church). As I sat on the grass, among thousands of other initiates, I felt like a small fish flapping on land. I'd never heard such talk. It was unimaginable that a decade later, the NGK would condemn apartheid as a sin. For the moment, however, it was the moral right that belonged to those in charge. I was in trouble!

CHAPTER 5

Intimidation

F ROM ABROAD, THE WHITE population of South Africa may have looked like a monolithic block, solidly bent on oppression, but it wasn't. It was composed of different groups and subgroups with much tension between them. At Onderstepoort, I would come up against the hard right wing of South African politics, and I would buckle at the intimidation. It was a shock to my system. I had grown up in a part of Johannesburg where the white residents were mostly at the progressive end of the political spectrum and, until I got to university, I hadn't encountered those who existed at the extremes of the other end, where racism was unapologetically blunt.

While white students lived in a hostel, the black students in our class had to live somewhere else, out of sight. During the day, when our class travelled between campuses, the white students went in a bus and the two black students followed in a Kombi van. When they were not invited to an important veterinary function, I organised a petition against their ongoing exclusion. A few people signed, but a counter-petition was soon circulated, crushing mine.

The dean called me in. It was unheard of that the great man would converse with a first-year student and there were whispers among my classmates that I was a dead man walking. I was petrified. Controlling his anger, the dean had me stand in front of his desk. He told me that because of my actions there would be no acceptance of any other black students at his faculty in the future. Then, from his drawer, he pulled out a wad of forms from black applicants, put it on the desk, picked up his fountain pen and crossed out names. He looked at me coldly: 'Just continue doing what you're doing, and I'll cross out more. Young man, listen very carefully to me. Either you shut your mouth, or you will be out of here as well.'

With that, he put the wad back in the drawer. I'd hit the iron wall of racism and felt powerless. Onderstepoort was an elite school, and the pressure was immense. We had nine lectures a day, an exam every week and the attrition rates were notoriously high. Although I was ranking well in class, after that encounter with the dean, my marks plummeted. I started getting exactly 49 per cent every week. Richard was terribly worried and begged me to toe the line and just try to pass. The situation was desperate when, without explanation, I started getting 51 per cent. This placed me exactly on the line and kept me at serious risk of dismissal. I was being softened up and, in the end, was successfully quietened on this score.

At the final oral exam for the year, I entered the room

and stood before a panel as directed. The external examiner on the panel stood up and started shouting, 'Call the senior examiner, this student is cheating.' I froze. The senior examiner came running. Pointing at me, my accuser proclaimed, 'We examined this very same student earlier this morning, and now he's back to try and get a better mark.' The senior examiner smiled. 'You are not completely wrong. He's an identical twin, but he's the difficult one.'

That was not completely wrong either. To celebrate the end of the year, a hostel at the University of Pretoria organised a Nazi-themed evening. Based on a famous meeting between Hitler and Mussolini, the hall was adorned with flags bearing swastikas and one student dressed as the German leader and the other as the Italian.

I didn't know about this until someone on the bus to Onderstepoort handed out copies of a student newspaper. Its front page displayed images from the dinner, including the Hitler character performing the Nazi salute. I was enraged and consulted with another Jewish student. We decided I should go and see the student leader at the hostel in question. He happened to be a local hero, captain of the university's first rugby team, six foot five, strong, proud and handsome. As there was a fair risk of us coming to blows, I asked the student to accompany me. A well-bred Afrikaner man would never be the first to strike if a woman was present.

We sat down at the entrance of the hostel to wait. Each hostel had its own meticulously kept rugby fields with facilities as spectacular as the American universities I'd seen in the movies. The hostel president appeared, listened to my complaint, and was dumbfounded that we found his event objectionable. He proceeded to lecture me in Afrikaans: 'You people must learn to forgive and forget. This occurred almost 40 years ago. We just had a theme for the dinner. And this was only a pretend event. What's wrong with you people? And how do we know this Holocaust occurred anyway?'

I replied that, with respect, six million people of mine died in concentration camps and gas chambers. Then I continued, 'You more than anybody should know about concentration camps because the first concentration camps were started by the British here, in South Africa. You know that 28 000 Afrikaner men, women and children perished in those camps.'

He cut me off before I could mention the 20 000 blacks who also died in the camps.

'You're *doodreg* [absolutely right]. It was a shocking thing that happened to them. We will never ever forgive the British.'

'But that was 80 years ago. How would you feel if we organised a dinner in celebration of Lord Kitchener with the Union Jack flying and us saluting a character dressed up like him as he strode into the hall?'

'That would never happen here. This is an Afrikaans university; that would be an absolute disgrace.'

'So can you not see how we feel?'

'No, I can't.'

He walked away abruptly. At that point, I went to a public phone booth and called the South African Jewish Board of Deputies. There was no support there. Afraid to draw attention to the Jews, a representative advised me there was nothing I could do and that I should leave it well alone. This did nothing to cool my hot head.

Without considering the consequences, I made another phone call, this time to the *Sunday Times*. That weekend, the paper carried the story on the front page, with photographs. There was nothing more to do. Professor Eduard Muntingh Hamman, the rector of the university, phoned the Board of Deputies to apologise and invited them to the campus to discuss the matter. They suggested he come to them. And, to his credit, he did.

When I look back at these episodes, they pale compared to what was happening to black people daily. I wasn't subjected to real intimidation. There was no threat of a severe beating, an arrest, a 90-day detention without trial (a South African favourite) or of my family being harassed. It was just a bit of pressure.

As the years at Onderstepoort passed, I knew I would never practise as a vet. I couldn't cope with the competing directives of the veterinary world. One minute you could be directed to do everything to save an animal's life, and a few minutes later you'd be requested to euthanise a perfectly healthy animal. I remember putting great effort into saving a puppy for a woman who was willing to pay for treatment, and then receiving 30 puppies, full of vigour and sweetness, from the SPCA. No home could be found for them, and it was my job to administer fatal injections, one at a time. As my interest in veterinary science was dying back, a different passion was taking its place.

Every Friday afternoon, Richard and I would drive back to Johannesburg and our first stop was the nursing home.

The week was over; we were in good spirits and hopeful of lifting our father's mood too. But our pleasure would often turn to anger at the neglect he endured. There were days when we could have put our fists in his open bedsores. We would bark at the staff, and they would respond because they knew we wouldn't leave unless they attended to him. But he never complained, and by the following weekend he was often in a grim state again.

As my enthusiasm about becoming a vet receded, so my desire to become a doctor grew. I wanted to become a doctor who could make a difference to patients' lives, and now I was in a hurry. Like Richard, I feared our father's disease would strike us too and that by 40 we would be incapacitated. Against all odds, our father hoped he might work again, so we never stopped working. He also hoped to walk and would say to us, 'Boys, one day I am going to walk from Cape Town to Cairo.' As he couldn't take a step, we ran. As schoolboys, we'd drop our bags with friends at the bus stop and then run the eight kilometres to school. As adults we ran whenever we could, and eventually we were running the 88-kilometre Comrades Marathon, the world's largest and oldest ultramarathon race.

In my third year at Onderstepoort, I went to Johannesburg to see Professor Phillip Tobias, the celebrated and much adored dean of the University of the Witwatersrand (Wits) medical school. I told him I wanted to switch to medicine. He leaned forward and asked why I hadn't done it in the first place. I explained. 'Don't be so judgemental,' he said. 'What you say may be true of some doctors but not all. That should never ever stand in your way.' It took me by surprise but, years later, I conceded that he was right.

I was judgemental, sometimes overly so, and I didn't care that people experienced me as harsh.

It was not insignificant to get that kind of advice from a man who had been nominated three times for a Nobel prize, was an outstanding opponent of apartheid, and regarded it as politically profound that life began in Africa. As a leading palaeontologist, he famously said that the colour of a person's skin was genetically of no scientific importance whatsoever.

Encouraged, I went to see the secretary of the medical school, who had a more conventional position: I should finish what I started, qualify as a vet, and then apply to medicine. I was turned down but not deterred.

In fourth year, I wrote a letter to Wits medical school saying something like 'I will become a doctor. This is my burning mission, and I don't intend to complete my veterinary studies. I assure you, I will make a positive contribution to medicine.' This resonated with somebody, and I was accepted into second-year medicine. Quite rightly, I lost all the financial support and the bursaries I was receiving for my veterinary degree and had to get a couple of jobs and take a loan until I managed to win scholarships.

Medical school was a revelation. From the first lecture, the fish was back in water. I was motivated and stimulated, and nothing was too much trouble. At lunchtime on that first day, I walked into the canteen on the ground floor and was astonished at the multiculturalism. People were chatting and eating at the same tables with an ease I didn't recognise. I kept thinking, 'I'm where I belong.' But I gradually realised that assessment was naive. Yes, it looked so different from Onderstepoort – and it was – but I wasn't seeing everything.

While we all got first-class training, when we got out into the field it was different. There were two health systems in the country, a wonderfully well-resourced one for whites and a very poorly resourced one for blacks. While white students could work in both systems, black students were not allowed in white hospitals, which had more advanced technology and where there were more staff and hours to do things differently. They were justifiably resentful, and at the end of our course they boycotted the class graduation photograph and arranged their own. They felt the medical school had not done enough or tried hard enough to reduce the restrictions imposed by apartheid and that their training had not been equitable. They were right. In those days, Wits medical school had a first-rate reputation and its graduates were welcomed around the world. That these students had not benefited in full was another infuriating missed opportunity. It was typical of apartheid, which somehow always got in the way.

But change was coming. In the following year, 1989, as part of a nationwide defiance campaign, demonstrators demanded blacks be admitted to white wards. Under normal public hospital policy, any black patients brought to a white emergency ward would be stabilised and then transferred to a black hospital, unless the person needed specialised treatment unavailable at the black hospital. This was iniquitous in so many ways. Hillbrow Hospital, the main black hospital in Johannesburg, had no paediatric or obstetrics facilities. This meant a child or pregnant woman had to travel 30 kilometres to Soweto, a township south of the city, while the grand General Hospital was nearby and had plenty of capacity.

In May 1990, three months after Madiba's release, the government announced it was opening South Africa's segregated public hospitals to all races. The sentiment was applauded but its application was slow. Many private hospitals, however, were already admitting black patients.

Richard had stayed on at Onderstepoort and completed his veterinary degree. He then put himself through a medical degree by working as a vet at an overnight emergency clinic. That we were identical – one working as a vet and one as a trainee doctor – caused some comic misunderstanding and consternation in the community.

I was on duty at the hospital clinic one morning when an elderly woman I had never seen before came up close and looked at my name tag.

'Ah, Dr Friedland, thank God it's you,' she said.

'Yes, thank God, but why? ' I asked.

'Why? Because I trust you. Don't you remember my dog? You treated him with such care.'

I was always doing extra work, and one Sunday morning, during a shift at the private Bagleyston Clinic, a woman came in with asthma. She looked at me quizzically. I treated her condition, but she was clearly uncomfortable and a bit suspicious. When it came to paying, she was reluctant. I put this down to the fact that I looked young and possibly inexperienced.

About two hours later, a car screeched to a halt outside the glass doors of the clinic. That same woman came rushing through the doors: 'I thought I knew you and now I know exactly who you are and I'm taking you to the medical council. Two weeks ago, you treated my cat and now you are masquerading as a doctor!' It took time to calm her down.

I showed her my ID card, explained that Richard was a vet, and eventually she got back into her car with her tail between her legs.

CHAPTER 6

Closer to the source

FROM THE MOMENT Madiba walked free, I was alive to him. I read everything related to him in the newspapers, and if he was mentioned on the radio, I turned up the volume and listened carefully. Was this man really going to deliver us from evil? The whole country was focused on him, the world was watching too, and he didn't seem to falter. There was no sign of a complex internal struggle and over time I forgot that one might even exist. Like everyone else, I began seeing him as pure hero. It was hard not to. He talked simply, honestly and with a dignity I'd not seen in a public figure before.

'Dignity' seemed to be one of the favourite words people used to describe him. I kept using it too, and as I observed him on the screen, I tried to understand what exactly was resonating with people. Yes, he had self-mastery, discretion, an appealing amount of self-confidence, a good reputation and was both respectful and charming, but there was something more. What was it?

It was a while before I noticed one of his unusual techniques. He would cut through the social hierarchy and level the ground between himself and others. He talked across, person to person, not down from a position of power.

At public functions, it was not unusual for him to break with protocol and go off to the kitchen to meet the staff and the cleaners. This wasn't a display of virtue because for him personhood had nothing to do with hierarchy. He wasn't having long conversations, but he was networking at a level that was not perceptible to others, and probably not to his impatient security guards. But those on the receiving end likely felt the difference.

He showed me that dignity is interactive. To be accorded dignity, you have to behave with dignity, and behaving with dignity means treating others with dignity, and when they feel they have been treated this way, they accord you the same. It's a virtuous circle, until it is broken. Over the years I would see Madiba angry and upset, but never without dignity.

But there was more than dignity. He operated in a different sphere and touched people at the level where the currents of intuition and faith run. He resonated at their frequency. My mother, who was very interested in the metaphysical world and took us into it too, described him as an 'old soul'. For her, there was no mystery. Like Gandhi, Madiba was one of the 'great souls' to walk the earth. While neither of these men were saints, she would say that in the latter periods of their lives they were closer to the source than the rest of us.

Madiba had become president a month ahead of his

seventy-sixth birthday, and as his five-year term progressed, age visibly crept up on him. You could see the burden of leadership was getting heavier. By then, I had developed a special interest in hearing problems and once I'd noticed that he wore hearing aids, I began concentrating on how well he was actually hearing. While others might have been watching him stride the world stage, I was closely watching his interactions, to see if and when he strained to catch what was being said.

At the time, it was very common for older men to hide a hearing deficit, but he was open about his loss. In a speech to adults and children who were hearing impaired, he talked of the barriers created by hearing loss and how, for many people, this 'can mean a special kind of loneliness'. Then, he talked of his own experience:

'I would like to tell you that I also wear hearing aids, just as you do. These little instruments made a big difference to my life. Wherever I go, they help me to listen better, to understand better.

'I would like to encourage you to wear your hearing aids as they will help you, especially to learn. Learning is your future, and it is the future of our country. Use this opportunity to help yourselves and your nation.

'It needs discipline to use a hearing aid. And to get the improvements in communication that make it possible requires the understanding, expertise, love and dedication of many people: family; friends; members of the community; teachers; and health professionals.'

Publicly, he was emphasising that using a hearing aid not only requires personal discipline but the understanding of those around you. This was exactly right.

Madiba diligently wore the hearing aids he'd been given after his release from prison in 1990 and was unconcerned about the stigma. He described them as one of the wonders of the modern age. In her memoir *Good Morning, Mr Mandela*, his long-term private aide Zelda la Grange says he had very few personal things 'that he was religiously holy about'. Among them were his pen, his reading glasses and his hearing aids, which meticulously had to be placed beside his bed every night.

As he approached his eighties, people began commenting that his hearing was deteriorating. The feeling was that this was age-related and to be expected. Given his stature, it was assumed he must be getting the best treatment, receiving the finest advice and that his hearing technology had probably reached the limit of its usefulness, so nothing more could be done. For his part, Madiba never complained. In the medical community, it was said he was loyal to his doctors, grateful for the care he received and respectful of their judgement.

As I watched him on the screen, I noticed that on a one-to-one basis, in the controlled environment of a television studio, he seemed fine. His exchange with the interviewer was fluid and his answers indicated he'd heard what was asked. But in a crowded room or a noisy press conference, he visibly struggled and would regularly request the question be repeated. Sometimes Zelda would relay it to him. She'd grown up as a white Afrikaner fully supporting apartheid and had been transformed by working with Madiba. Her devotion was well known, and in those days she could usually be found at his side or close by.

If he missed a complex exchange of conversation, he could look to her or someone else to summarise, but as many hearing-impaired people know, this doesn't substitute for the original. It's not just a case of passing on solid, compact, measured information. To hear what people say, you need to hear more than the words; tone, pitch, pace and the other subtleties in the mix of communication.

When there was a lot of noise and Madiba was on his own, sometimes his answers could be broad or obtuse to the point that people dismissed them as political obfuscation. But he was never one to avoid an issue. It wasn't his style. He said what he believed, regardless of the audience or the status of the individual he was addressing. Directness was one of his defining characteristics and, rather than being evasive, it seemed to me that he hadn't heard the question correctly and was trying to make do with the bits he'd grasped. With all his efforts concentrated on deciphering the words, he might have missed the nuances. Occasionally, I thought I could pick up his frustration.

I didn't know it, but the opportunity to talk to him about this directly was getting closer.

CHAPTER 7

See one, do one, teach one

F RESH FROM MEDICAL SCHOOL, I worked in the hospital system while it was still segregated and saw apartheid through a medical lens. The advantages for white patients were clear. They recovered from surgery in clean beds in modern hospitals with good facilities, state-of-the-art equipment and continuity of care.

Take the example of someone who had been shot. At the new Johannesburg General Hospital, the white victim would be brought in by ambulance, placed in their own resuscitation bay, assigned a surgeon and, after the operation, wake up in a sparkling ward. A full quota of nursing staff would be on duty, unhurried ward rounds would take place twice a day, and there would be immediate access to radiology, blood tests and anything else that was required in a setting of First World medicine.

It was different when I worked at Baragwanath, the

biggest hospital in Africa. It had once been an army barracks and by the mid-1990s was a sprawling collection of largely prefabricated single-storey buildings with outdoor corridors and corrugated-iron roofs. In summer it was hot as hell, and in winter the reverse. Overcrowding meant people often slept on the concrete floor.

Baragwanath was exclusively for black patients, and when you drove through you'd see people in hospital gowns sitting in the corridors or on the kerb, often smoking next to their drip stands. Those who didn't have stands carried their IV fluid bags on their heads as they walked. Some carried their urinary catheter tubes over their shoulders.

'Bara' served Soweto, then regarded as a separate township. It was part of the architecture of apartheid and had been designed in the 1930s to separate black people from white people. While the doctors were dedicated and had outstanding expertise, the volume of patients was so high that they worked without break. The volume also drew surgeons and physicians from around the world who wanted to help, to learn, but mostly to gain experience and improve their own skills.

The facilities, however, were poor. With no continuity of care, there was no personalised medicine. It was conveyor-belt medicine. Once a surgeon had extracted the bullet and repaired the tissue, there was no further involvement with that patient, because there was no time – someone else would follow up, sometime.

Over the weekend, Bara's emergency department was a warzone. It was nicknamed 'the pit' because trauma cases kept coming. Ambulances would queue to drop their injured, others were driven in by relatives, some walked in, and at any time there could be a line of a hundred patients waiting for access. Then there were more on trolleys, who couldn't stand. They had been triaged and each had a sticker on their forehead saying 'urgent'. They were waiting for a spot in the general resuscitation bay.

While much of the violence in Soweto was driven by poverty and alcohol, the easy availability of guns was changing the paradigm. If these hospital scenes had been filmed for a documentary, people would have questioned its veracity. In the surgical intake ward, it was not unusual for patients who had been freshly operated on for gunshot or stabbing wounds to sleep on the floor because all the beds were taken.

At any time over the weekend, there were up to eight trauma theatres at work. This meant there was little opportunity for the senior surgeons to supervise the trainees. While juniors hoped for ongoing supervision, the formula in the operating theatres and in 'the pit' was 'see one, do one, teach one'. In other words, you watched a particular procedure once, then you did one once, then you taught the next person how to do it. Proper training requires seeing many, doing many under supervision, and, when declared competent, teaching – and if you are diligent or academically inclined, publishing those cases that had novel characteristics.

More significantly, however, the formula served patients badly and – as I know from sad personal experience – was often dangerous. As a junior ENT trainee, I was instructed to remove a large growth in the middle ear of an adult man. The consultant was not present, and although I had never done a procedure with such extensive disease, I was told to operate solo. Although I was experienced at using a high-speed drill to get through the bone behind the ear, I lost my bearings. I cut through the facial nerve and paralysed half the patient's face. I realised immediately what I'd done. I unscrubbed and called the consultant, who was at home. He told me to close the wound.

The next day on a ward round, I presented the patient to the head of the department. He didn't need to berate me because my humiliation was complete when we all viewed the patient's face. Thankfully for the patient, and for me, the head of department immediately took the man back to theatre and reoperated on him, with me as his assistant. He regrafted the facial nerve. I trembled at the thought of the outcome, but a year later I saw the man and his face was normal. The graft had been successful, but he'd lost hearing on one side because of my lack of skill.

Although the hospital system was desegregated in 1990, change was slow and almost imperceptible in the emergency wards. As services across the country needed radical transformation, and as resources were limited, there was a kind of acceptance that nothing would happen fast.

After much indecision, I settled on specialising in ENT because I figured it would allow me to do a little clinical work, a little surgery, a bit of academic research and still have time for a decent family life. I would treat routine problems, have the occasional challenge, and be home for dinner.

I was wrong. The violence that had taken hold in South Africa turned me into a trauma surgeon. By then, guns were replacing knives and people were being held up in their cars. During these hijackings, many were shot through their car windows. As a result, I found myself working in a high-stress field that I would never have chosen. I had trained to perform tonsillectomies and sinus surgery and now I was reconstructing voice boxes, necks and ears shattered by bullets.

One Saturday evening, I was on call for Bara. I was a senior ENT registrar (trainee) at the time, and an ophthalmology registrar called to ask for my help. She was desperate. 'My consultant has been away the whole day and I have a patient who has been stabbed in the eye. Please come now.' I drove straight over, walked into the emergency department and there, lying in the corner, was a man with a large knife sticking out of his left eye. There was an 'urgent' sticker on his face.

'How long has he been lying like this?' I asked.

'About 14 hours,' came the reply.

'What happened?'

'He was sleeping, and his flatmate believed he had been betrayed. He suspected this man here [pointing] had been having a secret relationship with his girlfriend. So, he took out his flick-knife and stabbed him.'

It was staggering. He had not been treated sooner because he was breathing – he was alive, he was conscious, and importantly, he was stable. There were far more urgent cases that day and he was simply being triaged. An angiogram showed that the knife had missed the internal carotid, the major blood vessel to the brain, by millimetres. There was no one else to manage this case, so I took him to theatre with the ophthalmology registrar, and very carefully removed the knife. He lost his eye, but he survived.

Driving home, it struck me that had he been in the Johannesburg General Hospital, his dramatic injury would have been attended to immediately. An ophthalmologist, an ENT surgeon and a neurosurgeon would have rushed in, and he would now be a good 16 hours post-op. Perhaps there might have been a small chance of saving the eye. I remembered being taught that damage in one eye can affect the other. I didn't pursue that thought; it was too upsetting.

CHAPTER 8

Bullets

WITH MADIBA at the helm of the country, I thought I would never want to leave. But my faith in the future of the South Africa was seriously tested when three of my friends were shot dead, in three separate incidents, over 15 years.

Through this book, I describe each brutal incident as it happened. With each death, I weighed my loyalty to South Africa against my loyalty to my family and the visceral fear that my children would become fatherless. The first death occurred before I knew Madiba, and it sent me reeling in anguish and rage. The others took place later and set off an uncomfortable dissonance that stayed with me. Madiba had endured more than enough loss and violence for one man, yet he remained the calm centre of the nation. I'd visit his home, which was always serene, but I knew that outside his high walls the world was different and that this difference reached its extreme in the emergency department. Eventually, this discordance would compel me to make the most wrenching decision of my life, a decision in which not only my wife and family were involved but Madiba himself.

I'm told my exposure to violence in South Africa was not representative. Yes, I was pushed to the edge in the trauma unit, but what I experienced outside the hospital was not unusual for the era. Having been touched by violence, most people in the northern suburbs of Johannesburg were living defensively, but they still had to venture into unguarded public spaces. As it happened, all three of my friends met their deaths in parking lots.

The first incident happened in 1995, on my thirty-fourth birthday. Dr Stephen Pon had been my medical partner during the long years of ENT training. We studied together at my home, we worked together in the hospital, and if one of us couldn't make a shift, the other filled in. Our relationship was so seamless and collegial that on graduation we decided we'd get consulting rooms together.

At 31, Stephen was the youngest ENT surgeon in Johannesburg, with one of the highest qualifying grades. He was the third generation of a well-known family in Johannesburg's Chinese community. Stephen's grandparents had come to South Africa to be the principals of two local Chinese schools, one in Johannesburg and the other in Pretoria. His father, Henry Pon, was the first chartered accountant of Chinese ethnicity in the country.

To allow me to celebrate my birthday, Stephen delivered a lecture on my behalf to about 250 physiotherapy and occupational therapy students. That went well, and afterwards he went to see a patient at Johannesburg General Hospital. Around 4 pm, as he eased out of the doctors' car park, two youths posing as flower sellers flagged him down. They came up to his window, pulled out a high-calibre pistol and shot him in the chest. They wanted his new BMW 328i, a graduation gift from his parents.

A surgical trauma team worked on him for ten hours, and when they gave up, the cardiothoracic surgeon called me. I had no words. Doctors and nurses were mad with shock. Others of their number had died in hijackings, but it was the killing of a doctor in the hospital grounds that made this incident particularly shocking for them. If a doctor doing his duty in a public hospital was not safe, nobody was.

Although there would be about 8 000 hijackings in the province that year, what followed was unprecedented for a single case. Two large memorial services were held, the hospital's trauma unit closed for a day, and I marched with staff from several hospitals in protest. The message was that unrelenting violence was forcing us out of the country and South Africa was at risk of a brain drain that would take generations to recover. Henry Pon put it succinctly:

'Stephen was brought up in a family that was well disciplined, well educated and taught the value of life. But he had to move in a society where there are lots of people for whom life has no value. These youths grew up in the violence of the locations [townships] during white rule. As children they saw for themselves that life has no value, they saw people necklaced [killed with a burning tyre around the neck], they saw people shot or beaten to death. So, to them killing a person doesn't mean a thing. They have no conscience.'

It was the early days of Madiba's presidency, and although he had averted a civil war and made a relatively peaceful transition to majority rule, reversing the generational damage driven by apartheid would take decades. It had brutalised millions and affected everything, from family structures to moral consciousness and religious values. Children had lost respect for their parents, whom they regarded as too passive and too weak to challenge their oppressors. For the past 20 years, regardless of what their elders thought, these younger generations had taken radical political action. There had been so much dislocation and agony on both sides that no one knew how to rebuild regard for parents, family, authority and human life.

The post-election jubilation was mixed with nervousness and insecurity. It was a difficult time but there was hope. The shining promise was that, as his presidency progressed, Madiba would be able to settle the situation, narrow discrepancies and lead the country into prosperity.

Stephen's death was with me every time I entered the hospital grounds, and by 1997, I was unnerved by the daily toll in the emergency ward. Two or three times a week, I found myself dropping everything and rushing down the corridor to attend to a complex gunshot. As in Stephen's case, a whole team was needed to resuscitate a patient wounded by high-velocity rounds. While one forgets the details of the cases, what often remain are the non-cognitive aspects – the sight of brain fluid mixed with blood, the smells and the sounds. To maintain equilibrium I needed to debrief, and once a week I would have a counselling session. This helped, but the memories would surface unexpectedly. Most of the time I couldn't trace the trigger, but in one session it emerged that a particular shade of pink was linked to a particular flashback.

On Fridays, I used to wear a pink shirt. It was my private way of cheerfully marking the end of the week. I would finish early and be home in time to see Linda light the Sabbath candles, walk to synagogue with her and the children, and return to share a meal with the wider family. I was working at Milpark Hospital, where I had established an ENT department. My private consulting rooms were around the back of the hospital, and I was on call for emergencies. This top-tier private hospital was open to all races and took public patients too. If an ambulance brought a patient to Milpark, the patient was admitted.

Most unusual for a private hospital, it also had a level-one trauma unit that was as good as any in the world. It had a helipad and a highly skilled team, with a trauma surgeon and an anaesthetist present around the clock, every day of the week, and a support team permanently in place. One of its innovations was to scan emergency patients on their trolleys, as they were wheeled in. These scanners were adapted from those used in the local mining industry. As miners exited a mine, they usually passed through a frame that could detect gold or diamonds that might be on or in their bodies. Similarly, these hospital scanners could detect fractures and bullets, and locate them precisely. As many trauma patients were too unstable to be put in regular scanners, which took too much time, these devices gave emergency doctors a head start. Necessity had driven South Africa to adapt these scanners for hospital use. Despite the violence on the streets, doctors kept coming from abroad to train in trauma medicine.

One Friday morning I was in a particularly good mood. I'd been for an early ten-kilometre run with my running group and my endorphins were still high. We joked and laughed as we ran through the leafy northern suburbs of Johannesburg. We'd been doing this for years and I enjoyed the camaraderie. After a shower I put on my pink shirt. It would be a day of consultations, no surgery – easy! I told the family I'd be home at 3 pm.

I remember sitting at my cherrywood desk with a cup of coffee, chatting to a patient about a tonsillectomy, when I was buzzed. It was the trauma coordinator: Code One – gunshot, face and neck. Code One was the highest emergency and there could be no delay. It was a short run from my consulting rooms to the trauma theatre, and as I dashed away my receptionist took over. She informed my patients that there had been a shooting, rebooked everyone and cleared the waiting room. Violence was so common that people understood. They accepted it in the way pregnant women in a waiting room accept their appointment being delayed because the gynaecologist suddenly has to rush off to attend to a birth. If they were in labour, they'd want the same.

By the time I got there, the patient's clothes had been cut off, and as he bled out, so he was being pumped with blood. The trauma surgeon and the anaesthetist were at work, and others were arriving. We were still in the golden hour for survival and once the vascular surgeon had stemmed the patient's bleeding and he was temporarily stabilised, we paused to discuss strategies.

This policeman had been shot in Yeoville, an inner-city suburb of Johannesburg. Somehow, we knew that he and a colleague had responded to a call for help and the colleague had been killed. He was bending over this man's body when someone came from behind and took his gun. As he turned to look, he was shot in the head. Then he was shot in the chest.

By the time I saw him he had swabs in his mouth. His tongue was lacerated and hanging through the cheek, and he was still bleeding through the back of his neck. From the scans, we knew there was a bullet to the back of his skull, and from an exit route we could see another had gone through his chest and out the other side.

Our priority was to stabilise the carotid and jugular arteries in the neck, but we were concerned about neuro-vascular trauma. Damaged blood vessels can be managed but damage to the nerves can be hard to detect and can cause functional problems later. For 12 hours we worked on him. It takes that long because we all wait in the theatre as each specialist does their part. It's a flat structure and we assist each other while watching closely because it will affect what we each will do, or what we have just done. This is teamwork and no one leaves the theatre for more than a few minutes at a time.

Once I had repaired his tongue and palate, a maxillo-facial surgeon worked on his jaw and a plastic surgeon on his cheek. With that done, we operated on the area where the jugular vein enters the skull and stemmed any remain-ing bleeding. At the same time, the cardiothoracic surgeon was draining his lungs and evacuating the clots. This work is tough, but you are so absorbed you don't notice how many hours are passing. I did remember to step outside to phone Linda to say I'd be home very late that night. I was in a constant battle of priorities between my patients and my family. Something had to give and usually it was the family. I steeled myself against both their disappointment and any discomfort I might feel about missing important events. But by then, I was beyond explaining. The relativities of the situation in front of me made it impossible to walk away. On the table was an otherwise healthy man in his twenties. He'd been doing an essential job and now his life hung in the balance.

By the time we got him back to the ICU ward, his family had arrived, and it fell to me to talk to them. I saw this small, shocked group of his closest relatives huddled outside the ward. They had little understanding of modern medicine and asked no questions. I had a social worker and translator with me and tried to explain in simple terms what we had done to keep him alive. They didn't seem to register. They just looked at me.

They waited and eventually, one at a time, were allowed to go to his bedside for a few moments. His face was a mess, but we'd bandaged it, and he had tubes coming out everywhere. The last thing I saw was his very young wife, with her head in her hands. It was time for me to go.

CHAPTER 9

The pink shirt

HANGING IN A LOCKER, my pink shirt didn't look so cheerful any more. As I buttoned it up, I could not have imagined this shade of pink would embed itself in the primitive part of my brain. Any hint of it would catapult me back to this young policeman and his broken throat. On the way home I thought about how his ability to swallow and speak would be severely affected. More than anything, he needed help and hope.

A few days later, when he was fully present, I promised him he would speak and swallow again. Given the damage to his neck, my colleagues thought I was overpromising. In medical school, we were taught to practise defensive medicine, so-called 'cover your arse medicine'. It means discussing every possible complication, even those with only a one per cent chance of occurring. This prudent medico-legal approach would have you say, 'We will have to wait and see.'

But this does not take the power of the human psyche into account. Most of us have seen recoveries that go beyond the bounds of science, and while I agree that patients need to know the realities, they also need hope. With long-term, committed rehabilitation, I believed this policeman would not get back to where he was before the shooting, but that he would achieve enough function to swallow, talk and live well enough. For many patients, the doctor is the drug. If the doctor is fully present and listens, without interrupting or looking at a screen, this can be healing in itself. The gift of presence is tremendously valuable and, although patients may not know it, it works in reverse too. Doctors receive something from their patients' presence, just as I did from this policeman.

He entered my psyche and I will always remember him. I'd done a tracheotomy, and while the tube normally comes out after a week to ten days, his swelling was so persistent that it remained in place for six months. As he was unable to swallow, a feeding tube went into his stomach. For six months he couldn't talk, not only because of his tongue but because the nerves to his voice box were destroyed and the swelling wasn't helping. He became depressed.

Over the months, we built trust, and this kept a small light burning. I looked him directly in the eyes and kept reassuring him that when all the tubes were out and we had rebuilt his voice box, we would teach him to speak and swallow again. He understood and wanted to believe me. And so it happened: after many months of incremental rehabilitation with a team of experts, he began to regain function. I followed him the whole way, explaining the small steps. His problem was not just structural, it was that the sensation had gone from the left side of his face, neck and throat. He couldn't sense food on that side, and it would just drop down his gullet, which could be dangerous. Using thickened fluids and other methods, the team trained him to turn his head so he could swallow on the right side.

By the end, he was able to eat very slowly and with concentration, but this would improve. He looked normal again and regained a hoarse but audible voice. Shortly afterwards he wrote me a letter of appreciation on a piece of paper, torn from a notebook. English wasn't his home language, but sincerity shone from the page. Then he wrote telling me he and his wife had just had a baby and inviting me to a party at his house to welcome the child. Although he gave me good directions to navigate my way through Soweto, I got lost among the small shacks and modest houses. When I arrived at the gathering, everyone was taken aback. He'd probably invited the rest of the team, but I was the only one present and they treated me as an honoured guest. He wasn't perfect, but he was back, and as I watched him, with the baby, surrounded by family and members of his church, I felt a lump in my throat.

I had operated on dozens of patients in the intervening months, but I remembered working inside his mouth and feeling an intense closeness to him. His was one of those rare cases where you enter the greater stream of humanity. If I had told this to my colleagues, most would have thought I was nuts. I never talked about this to anyone, and the policeman wouldn't have known it, but he responded to it with his full presence and trust. In his way, he let me into his life.

But around this time, another man let me into his life too, and ultimately I disappointed him. He wasn't a patient;

he was a prisoner serving a life sentence in a maximum-security jail. The prison complex needed the services of an ENT surgeon and I volunteered. For some six years, I held a clinic in the prison every second Thursday morning. This man, Ernest, was working in the sick bay, and over time a connection built between us. He was in his forties and had been behind bars for half his life. Having grown up without parents or schooling, he described his young self as a delinquent. As part of a gang, he'd robbed a bank. People had died, and although he was now paying for their lives, there was a lightness of being in him.

Prison, he said, had given him time to think about what he'd done and to find a way to reform himself. More than anything, he wanted to become 'a good person' and he believed studying would help. He was open, he liked me, and I liked him – in some ways like an older brother. I used to look forward to going to the prison, always hoping he was on the roster that Thursday morning. He would ask about my family. I knew that, sadly, none of his brothers or sisters visited him any more.

He told me that a few years earlier, during riots in the jail, the prison library had burned down and there was no reading material to be had. I sought and received permission from the head of the prison to build a new library together with Ernest. The prison would provide the space and the shelving, and I would provide the books.

My first stop was my mother. In her latter years she had moved from teaching to running the school library and was extremely enthusiastic about this project. She knew how to source excess books and secured a thoughtful mix of about 2 000 titles. For months, at every visit I would bring a car boot full of boxes. The authorities checked them and passed them on to Ernest, who was in charge of the emerging library. He became the permanent librarian and wrote me and my mother beautiful notes of appreciation. My mother was keen to visit the library and help him to create a catalogue, but that was not allowed.

I wouldn't have wanted her to go anyway. The prison was built into a hill, and once inside you descended underground to the dank cells. This facility was only for black men. It had no natural airflow; it was crowded and depressing. Prisoners washed the green cement floors with disinfectant soap and the whole complex smelt of it. For the rest of my life, if ever I got a whiff of that acrid smell, this jail would come to mind.

While some of the prisoners who came to see me were just looking for a change of scenery and were not ill, over the years many needed operations and I would add them to my patient list at a nearby hospital. While the men didn't necessarily welcome their surgery, they loved the hospital sojourn. Treats or small gifts were not permitted, and I was forbidden from improving their stay in any way.

But concerns about safety were bringing my visits to the prison to an end. The complex was understaffed, occasionally I noticed gates were left unlocked and, although it might have been my paranoia, I could feel a deterioration in the atmosphere. While my mobile phone and my instruments had extra value in that environment, I was worried about my life. My colleagues, who had had declared me mad to work there in the first place – it was dangerous and the remuneration was pitiful – said I should just walk away. I couldn't.

So I stayed and noticed more security lapses. Although

some were minor, I felt vulnerable. Then it happened. A violent riot broke out and I was trapped in the sick bay. After some hours a security squad found me and escorted me out. That was it. I felt terrible about abandoning the patients, but I never went back. The medical records were up to date, intact and accessible so my successor, if there was to be one, could take over.

I can't say what happened to Ernest. I never said good-bye and I never thought to write to him. In the previous riot he'd lost his books, and in this one he'd lost me. In those days HIV/AIDS was rife in male prisons and antiretro-viral medication was not made available to those who were infected. This meant the mortality rate among prisoners was shockingly high. That's what I tell myself.

CHAPTER 10

What the patient hears
(and sees)

AMID ALL ITS TROUBLES, South Africa was capable
of greatness. The world watched in awe as it went
through the catharsis of the Truth and Reconciliation Commission, which aired atrocities committed by
agents of the government and liberation movements during
apartheid. Testimonies were taken from many thousands of
victims, and applications for amnesty were made by thousands of perpetrators. The nation was reaching for healing
and restoration, and while the process was not perfect, many
of those who had suffered were finally given a voice.

But during the commission and in its aftermath, violence in the country did not stop. It was almost endemic,
and I'd be at home watching a heartbreaking account from
the commission while the trauma unit was calling to request
my urgent attendance. This wasn't a call to deal with mass
violence, just individual, ruthless and deadly crime. One

Sunday afternoon, a couple of kilometres from my house, a woman was sitting in her car waiting for her son when she was shot in the throat. The gunmen dragged her onto the road, robbed her, then left her for dead as they sped away in her car. Her throat was so damaged the paramedics couldn't insert a breathing tube and rushed her to the trauma unit at Milpark.

An expert trauma surgeon was waiting for her, and, thinking she was unconscious, without an anesthetic he created an emergency airway just below the bullet hole. While doing this, he commented to the team that this woman would never speak again. He didn't know it, but she was awake, gurgling and fighting to breathe. She heard that pronouncement and it seared itself in her memory.

When it comes to survival, the most primitive human reflex is to protect the airway, because without breath, there is no life. To maintain breathing, the oldest layer of the brain, the reptilian brain, recruits every instinct and for a brief time can give that patient superhuman power. I learned about this 'final fight' at medical school, but what I didn't learn was that in this hyper-charged state, the patient's memory can be heightened too.

My phone rang. By the time I got to the hospital the patient was in the theatre, unrecognisable. My job was to reconstruct her throat and her shattered voice box. I opened her neck and then dissected what was left of the voice box, spreading it open like a book. This way, I could sew the vocal cords and other structures back together with micro-stitches.

To help it heal, I inserted a temporary stent (device) and closed the box around it. This smart stent would stay in place for six weeks before being removed through the mouth. Only then would we know how successful the operation had been; only then would we know if she had a voice. For many patients, these six weeks can be emotionally rocky. As an organ of the soul, the voice is an expression of identity. Without it, we are reduced.

The next morning, I received an email from a doctor in America. In part, this is how it read:

Dear Peter,
I'm writing this email with a heavy heart. My beautiful sister, [name withheld], was shot in the neck while sitting in the car in broad daylight ...

Now she is in Milpark trauma unit. I would really appreciate it if you could stop by – as a friend to me – and without stepping on any toes, just let me know how things are. I keep thanking God that she survived, and I'm praying she will recover...

... Anything you can do to advise will be so much appreciated. Please email me a time to call you.

I'd met this doctor once a few years before, but I remembered him immediately because, at the time, we'd both felt a connection and we remarked upon it. I explained that she was already my patient and said I would keep him updated. After a few days of processing what had happened, his sister became increasingly aggressive. She didn't want my medical help and she didn't want my concern. Without knowing that she had heard and taken the surgeon's words as gospel, I was encouraging her about the future, saying I expected she would talk again. She was lying flat, physically uncomfortable and generally out of sorts, and I could see that the inability to voice her rage was intensifying her fury. There was something familiar about this. I think it touched the old story that lived in me. In the early stages of his disease, my father raged against his circumstances too. The difference was that, now, I was no longer a boy.

At ten days I wrote to her brother:

> The euphoria and relief of being alive have quickly dissipated into the anger and frustration that go with reality. This is entirely justified and warranted. She told me yesterday (in a handwritten note) that I don't need to see her again, and that my visits are totally unnecessary. She'll be fine!
>
> I told her that she's 'full of shit', and until she can tell me, without the stent, 'to piss off', I will always be around. That put a smile on her face – some sense of humour!

This woman went through serious ups and downs. I organised good accommodation for her in the hospital and, as she could sip fluids, suggested she walk to the hospital coffee shop for a cappuccino. As the weeks passed she struggled, and there were times when she didn't want to live. At one point, I gave her a CD player so she could listen to tranquil music with guiding healing imagery. When she suffered an unrelated medical setback, I requested she be placed in an ICU adjacent to my consulting rooms.

Too many things were going wrong, and I remember her not wanting to wear hospital pyjamas. So I gave her big, capacious shirts that could fit over all her tracheotomy gear. These were the shirts my running group wore. In fact, runners all over South Africa wore them although they had nothing to do with running. They were just a 'thing' and even non-runners wanted them. The shirts had a little fox on the front, and at the back they read, 'We do it cleanly'. They were made and handed out by my friend Gerald Fox, who manufactured cleaning rags. More about him later. I gave her at least one red shirt because, in so many cultures, red is regarded as a powerful colour. Some believe it brings luck, some think it wards off the evil eye, and others trust it can give courage and even help to burn out disease. She loved the shirts. I wish I had been able to make my father feel comfortable and loved as well.

All through the six weeks, I kept telling her she would speak again. Intuitively, I felt she would regain some voice. This was not a scientific assessment and, again, I was taking a risk. But without that risk, there would be no hope. When the time came to remove the stent, the procedure went relatively smoothly. We wheeled her to the recovery room where, for the first time since the shooting, we wanted her to use her airway. Standing next to her, I said, 'I'm going to call your brother so you can talk to him.' She glowered at me, shook her head, waved her forefinger, made a fist, indicating to everyone in the room – without any ambiguity – that I should not call.

So I called. It was 3 am for him and his wife answered. She said he'd had a very busy night, and she wasn't prepared to wake him. I introduced myself, said I was from South Africa and that he would be very upset if I didn't wake him. He came to the phone. 'I've got someone who wants to speak to you,' I said. Then I put my cellphone to her ear.

'Hello, my darling,' she said in very hoarse but recognisable voice.

He cried, she cried, I cried and everyone in the recovery room cried.

At this point, I want to confess that I had a reputation as a very demanding and difficult young surgeon. I never shouted or threw instruments, but when there was tardiness or indifference in theatre, others could feel the heat coming off me. I put myself and the theatre staff under pressure. While I could be a warm and considerate doctor, I could also burn people with my expectations. I was not popular, but I survived.

So when this woman used to scowl at me and give me vulgar hand signals to get out of her room, I took no offence; I understood. With age, however, I got better at hearing the feedback from my surgical colleagues and the theatre nurses and tried to manage my frustrations more effectively. It was always a work in progress. My reputation never really improved and the view of me as expecting too much from too many people persisted. I was, and I think I still am, driven by that old story.

There was so much for me to learn about emergency medicine. Just as you can't always tell what a patient hears, sometimes you don't know what they see. This came home to me in unexpected circumstances.

There is a religious Jewish festival, Shavuot, that involves studying through the night to sunrise. On one such occasion, I was going to lead the study group at our synagogue and Linda was going to make us all dinner beforehand. Well prepared and looking forward to the event, I was almost dressed when our landline began ringing. As I wasn't on call, I let it ring. When it rang out, it started again. Then again. So I picked it up.

It was the coronary care ICU unit at Milpark Hospital. After being given a particular drug to dissolve clots in his heart, an older man had begun to bleed though his nose, mouth and ears and elsewhere. The cardiologist on call, and his deputy, couldn't be reached. Neither could any of the other cardiologists on their list.

'But why call me? I'm not a cardiologist,' I protested.

'Because we know you will come.'

Linda begged me not to go, saying I would let the group down and she would have to host the dinner alone. I was torn. I wanted to stay, but I couldn't help myself. An old imperative clicked in and I got into my car and drove to the hospital. As had happened so often before, once inside the hospital, the resentment evaporated and my professional self took over. I suspended thoughts about what I was missing. As I entered the cardiac ICU, I saw a grey-haired man in a separate cubicle opposite the nursing station, unconscious, surrounded by nurses. They didn't want to give him an antidote to the drug because they feared he might clot, and that would cause additional heart problems. So I began procedures to manage the bleeding. He needed an airway, but I couldn't do a tracheotomy because the risk of his bleeding into it was too high. So I spent the night manually suctioning the blood out of his mouth and throat, using ice cubes and packs to reduce bleeding, and constantly swabbing any excess. It got easier as the drug began to wear off.

Towards sunrise, I was relieved and went home to collapse. I telephoned later that day to hear he was on the mend. With that, he left my mind and I moved on.

About two years later, I was at a religious Jewish wedding where the men dance together. My brother and I are usually instrumental in dragging others onto the floor and upping the pace. It would get so intense and sweaty that we got into the habit of taking spare shirts to the venue. This night, when the music momentarily stopped, an older man I didn't know came up to me.

'Will you dance with me?' he asked.

'What do you mean "will I"? I'd love to.'

'You don't know why I'm asking?'

'No.'

'Well, I didn't know who you were, but when you walked onto the dance floor and I saw your face and your eyes, I knew you.'

'Where from?'

'I was in trouble in ICU. I heard the nurses on the phone for an hour, ringing doctors to ask them to come and help me. No one came and I thought, "That's it, I'm going to die here." The last thing I saw was your face as you walked towards me. I wanted to write to you, but you left no trace. Why didn't you send me an account? To this day, I never knew who you were.'

'I remember! It was Shavuot.'

'Yes, it was, so?'

'Whenever I help someone on a *chag* [religiously significant day], I take it as a blessing. That's why I never put a sticker on your file.'

He took my hands and asked, 'Do you know whose

wedding this is?'

'Of course!'

'Do you know who I am?'

'No.'

'I'm the grandfather of the bride.'

We embraced, we cried, we danced together and when others heard the story of this odd couple on the floor, they joined us.

Although I had thought he was unconscious, imperceptibly he'd seen me. From this and other experiences, I think it may be that the acute awareness of those 'last' moments are not stored in one's working memory but are permanently imprinted in the depths of one's reptilian brain.

CHAPTER 11

The second phone call

O N HIS RELEASE, Madiba was given a pair of hearing aids that he went on to wear throughout his presidency. With age, people naturally lose hearing in the higher frequencies, and this reduces their ability to understand speech against background noise. They can hear the sounds but have difficulty making out meaning. It's similar to the clatter of a cocktail party that leaves guests – even with good hearing – straining to catch the conversation. This loss is gradual, ongoing and invisible to others. It can be so slow that many don't realise what they are missing, or even that they have difficulty hearing. They may no longer hear birdsong but remain unaware that it is missing.

For Madiba, the decline was likely exacerbated by noise-induced hearing loss. His first 18 years on Robben Island were spent not just as a prisoner, but as a prisoner of noise. For the first few years he would spend his days breaking up stone with a hammer and chisel in the prison courtyard. Then it got worse. He and the other prisoners were moved to a limestone quarry where they had to use a pick and shovel to break large stones into smaller ones to be used as road pavers. This was noisy work, and the relentless banging no doubt affected their ears.

We damage our hearing by exposing ourselves to very high decibels for a long time, which is worsened by being very close to the source of the noise. Instinctively, we distance ourselves from noxious sources of noise, but as these men were trapped, damage was inevitable and accumulated over time.

They knew their eyes were at risk from the sunlight reflected by the limestone and eventually received poor-quality dark glasses for protection. But, by then, many had suffered irreparable damage to their eyes too. After Madiba's release, press photographers were asked not to use a flash because it would further impact his retinas.

Towards the end of his presidential term, I noticed that his hearing had become a real issue and it seemed to me that there was a good chance that upgrading his technology might help.

At the time, I was at Milpark Hospital and regularly found myself working alongside the doyen of respiratory physicians, Professor Mike Plitt. He also happened to be Madiba's personal physician. By chance, Mike and I had both bought into a holiday development on the South Coast, in KwaZulu-Natal. Mike's large house was beautifully located, overlooking the beach. I was the proud owner of a fifth of a share of a villa up the side of the estate. San

Lameer was an easy car ride from Johannesburg, and whenever our time-share came up, Linda and I would pile our kids (by then our family had grown to five children) into an SUV, attach a trailer and drive down.

It was customary to walk around the grounds of this 200-hectare golf estate, and through bumping into Mike and chatting outside the hierarchy of the hospital, something in our relationship relaxed. One evening on his terrace, I cautiously raised the subject of Madiba's hearing and asked if his ears were being routinely checked. 'Yes, of course they are,' said Mike indignantly. 'He has an ENT guy he visits regularly, who cleans out his ear wax and looks after his hearing in general.' I pressed on regardless, describing what I had observed on TV and then turning to the matter of his hearing aids.

'Mike, I don't want to step on anybody's toes,' I said, 'but he's using outdated technology.' When hearing aids first came out, they were just glorified speakers. Each contained a microphone that captured noise and blasted it into the ears unchanged, but at a higher volume. They were to the ears what off-the-shelf magnifying spectacles are to the eyes – enhancers without customisation to the specific needs of the user. Just as the cheap spectacles made everything big, so these devices made everything loud.

To improve speech discrimination, it is more effective to boost higher-frequency sounds – specifically those frequencies that have been shown on a hearing test to be deficient in the user – than it is to boost lower-pitched sounds. In fact, enhancing lower-frequency sounds unnecessarily might interfere with speech discrimination, by adding unwanted noise. From what I'd seen on television, Madiba's hearing aids made life manageable for him on a one-to-one basis but were no longer helpful in other, particularly crowded, situations.

Without being emphatic, I suggested he might benefit from the latest digital hearing technology that had been available since the late 1980s. Mike acknowledged my suggestion, passed me a beer and we changed the subject.

Several months later, I was at home, pottering around the garden on a Sunday afternoon, when Mike called. It was about 3 o'clock. 'Peter, would you mind going to see Madiba. He's awfully frustrated because he can't hear. He and Graça [his new wife, Graça Machel] have just landed in a helicopter from Maputo [Mozambique], and I think he needs to have wax removed.' The helicopter had just set down on the playing fields of the Old Edwardian sports club in Houghton, about 300 metres from Madiba's house. The sooner I could go, the better.

Would I mind? I'd been waiting for such a moment.

In fact, I'd missed the previous moment. A year before, I was at San Lameer when Mike called my rooms to ask if I'd see Madiba. My receptionist had said I was on holiday and, without telling me, referred Madiba to my junior associate. Had I known, I would have flown back.

Wanting to look presentable, I dressed in smartish pants and a crisp shirt, and packed my headlight, a little ENT kit, an ear curette and some other basic equipment. Then I headed for Houghton, a suburb less than five kilometres away.

Houghton had been developed around the turn of the

twentieth century as a suburban sanctuary for well-to-do whites. It was not unusual for other folks to take a Sunday afternoon drive through its jacaranda-lined avenues to look at the mansions, many built in the modern style of Le Corbusier. Towards the end of the century, however, the low garden fences that once allowed these homes to be displayed to their best advantage had been replaced with tall walls and motorised gates for security, only sometimes allowing a glimpse of what lay beyond. As apartheid was dismantled, so was the white monopoly of this sought-after suburb.

In the car, my heart was beating with joy. I was about to see the hero of South Africa and my personal hero. Madiba and Graça had taken occupation of this Houghton house after they married on his eightieth birthday, and now that his presidency was over, it was their Johannesburg base.

As far as I could see, there was no sign on the Houghton house, and after parking outside its high walls, I walked over to a bulletproof glass cubicle where I introduced myself through a video phone. After I had been scanned, had my identity checked and explained what I was doing there, my possessions were carefully examined and scanned separately. Finally, I was directed up a short and narrow driveway towards the house. I passed Madiba's car, a black stretch BMW 750iL with thick bulletproof wheels and windows. Two other black BMWs and an ambulance stood nearby, all part of his standard convoy.

As I reached the grand entrance of the old mansion, I paused to collect myself and commit the moment to memory. Then I mounted the stairs, towards an enormous set of double wooden doors that lay open to the warm afternoon. All was quiet. Inside I could see a hall table bearing an abundance of flowers, and a huge portrait of Madiba and Graça on the wall.

I didn't know what to do. There was no bell and no one to be seen. Should I knock? I did. No response. I took a step into the house and saw sliding doors to a large lounge area. As I turned, what looked like two big white leather chairs came into view. In my state of heightened awareness, they looked like thrones.

And there was Madiba, sitting on one of them like an emperor, wearing his glasses and reading the newspaper. On a small table lay his pen and his spectacle case. The afternoon light, pouring through two sash windows, framed this surreal scene.

Spellbound, I stepped a little closer and cleared my throat, but he couldn't hear it. So, I said, 'Madiba' and he looked up at me, his face breaking into a smile. 'I'm terribly sorry to disturb you,' I said. 'My name is Dr Peter Friedland. I'm an ENT doctor and Dr Plitt asked me to come and see you.'

In the slow, deep voice I would come to know, he said, 'Ah, doctor, I'm so grateful that you have come to see me. Thank you for giving up your time. I'm just an old man and it is very kind of you to come.'

I went to him, and he put out his hand. It was big and warm and as I held it, I was trying not to cry.

Sitting on a small chair next to him, I explained I would like to help him with his ears.

'Doctor, I'm not able to hear things; even those things I'm supposed to hear, I'm not able to hear.'

'Madiba, would you mind if I examined your ears?' I couldn't believe I was actually touching this giant of a human being, who was sitting quietly in his beautiful, patterned shirt, radiating something I'd not experienced before. It felt like a dream.

I gently took out a hearing aid that was truly 20 years old. It was a museum piece. I could see his ear was impacted with wax. If the other ear was this bad, it was no wonder he couldn't hear because even a person with normal hearing would struggle. I realised in that moment that his hearing loss was being managed like most other people's hearing loss – with resignation and acceptance.

As I started my work, I felt my face flush, aware that I was performing an intimate procedure – albeit a very minor one – on one of the greatest living human beings. Wearing a headlight to guide my instruments, very slowly and carefully I removed the clumps of wax. When I could finally see his ear drum, even without putting in his hearing aid, his face shone with gratitude and astonishment at how well he could hear on that side. When I did the same on the other side, he lit up. 'Now, doctor, I am going to hear all the things I should not be hearing.' This was a phrase he would repeat every time I cleaned his ears or when the audiologist I worked with adjusted his hearing aids. When I showed him the wax I'd removed and explained it was dark because it had been there a long time, he was interested and relieved.

Then I tested each hearing aid. It's a very simple test. You put it in the palm of your hand and cup it, and if there's feedback, you hear ringing. There was no sound at all. The batteries in both were flat. While his staff looked for new batteries and found the very last set in the house, I cleaned out the wax that was clogging the miniature tubes of the hearing aids.

While he encouraged others to be disciplined in order to benefit from their hearing aids, and while he used his own diligently and guarded them carefully on his bedside table, he no longer had the capacity to maintain them himself. Perhaps everyone was distracted by his busy schedule, and the loss of this important function had been relegated to a less than urgent issue.

When I put them back in his ears, he gave me the smile that had touched hundreds of millions of people around the world and had melted the hearts of dictators. 'Ah doctor,' he said, 'I'm very happy now.'

CHAPTER 12

Where's the evidence?

A T MIKE PLITT'S REQUEST, I began visiting the house every four to six weeks when Madiba was in Johannesburg. When not travelling internationally, he and Graça spent time at her home in Mozambique or in the Eastern Cape in Qunu, the little village that he called home and where he'd enjoyed the happiest moments of his childhood as a herd boy.

The more I went to the Houghton house, the more familiar I became with the staff, and sometimes I'd enter through the kitchen door, drawn in by the smell of the lamb curry he regularly had for lunch. I met Zelda on my second or third visit and found her calm, matter-of-fact, controlling, in charge of access to Madiba and entirely devoted to him. On my third visit I met Graça, who welcomed me warmly and was engaging and grateful that I was taking care of her husband's hearing. I'd managed to secure a year's worth of batteries for the house and, over time, trained one of the housekeepers, Sarah, to change them and clean the hearing aids. She accepted the task and did it well.

Although Madiba's hearing was temporarily restored and a little improved in crowds, we weren't there yet. Two challenges lay ahead. The first was to get him to use a new-fangled Bluetooth device at meetings. The other was to get him to carry a spare set of hearing aids in case the first set became problematic while he was travelling. I never expected he might object to these suggestions.

After visiting Madiba at his home for more than a year, it was clear to me that although we were managing to keep his hearing aids in good working order, we also needed to upgrade his technology. This was a delicate matter. Observing protocol, I raised the subject with Mike Plitt. In a conversation about the general state of Madiba's health, I asked to see records of his previous hearing assessments. Mike didn't have any records.

In the dozen or so years since his release, he must have had an assessment, at least when he received his hearing aids. Perhaps the results were confidential. As president, he would have had regular health check-ups and these would have included routine ear examinations, but whether he had received diagnostic hearing assessments was unknown.

It is very common for hearing loss to go unattended, particularly in older men. While many men don't, or don't want to, acknowledge this loss, I knew Madiba was different. He was meticulous about attending to his health and wanted to maintain it at the best level possible, regardless of the effort involved.

Mike wasn't enthusiastic about a hearing assessment,

saying there were many other demands on Madiba's time and this didn't seem necessary. It would require too much organisation, complicated logistics and too much time. There was no question about his dedication to Madiba's wellbeing, but maximising hearing was a not a priority in the medical mindset of the moment, and anyway, I had no hard evidence. Mike was a scientist and had to be convinced. But over a year, I wore him down until he gave me permission to proceed with a full assessment.

At the time, I was also thinking about a quirk in the way that hearing aids are perceived, and how this further handicaps the wearer. When you see a person with a white stick, it's a powerful symbol; you understand immediately that they are sight-impaired, and you make appropriate allowances. At first glance, you would think a hearing aid would be a clear symbol too, but it's not.

It signals that the person has recognised their impairment and is managing it, but it doesn't mean their problem is fixed. Their hearing may be improved but they might still have difficulty hearing everything that you hear. As the name of these devices suggests, they aid hearing and are not substitutes for hearing.

Background noise has always been the most disturbing factor in understanding speech, and for some people who wear the devices, even a face-to-face conversation can be a challenge if there is ambient noise. The common assumption that hearing aids enable people to hear normally in all situations is often the reason others don't make any allowances for them in conversation. So, if people were going to assume Madiba could hear because he was wearing hearing aids, I felt it very important that he have the best possible option.

In those days, I worked with Shamim Ebrahim, a highly experienced and respected speech pathologist in Johannesburg. In South Africa at the time, it was unusual for a Muslim woman and a Jewish man to be working in a professional partnership together, but we did so collegially and with mutual respect. We ran a hearing clinic out of my rooms at Milpark Hospital and conducted research too. When I told her about Madiba's issue and asked if she would test his hearing, she became quiet. Then she cried. Being classified as 'non-white' in South Africa, Shamim and her family had suffered a lifetime of cruel discrimination. Madiba had led the movement that freed them from this and the thought of meeting him overwhelmed her.

Arrangements were made with his minders to bring him to the hospital, but because of security issues they couldn't tell us when he would come. It was 2003, he was still travelling a lot, and as he appeared to make do with his hearing, no one else regarded it as a pressing issue.

Madiba never complained and sometimes joked about it, as he did when Michael Parkinson arrived to interview him at home that same year. As Parkinson tells it, the crew was all set up and he had his back to the door when the room went quiet. Then he heard Madiba say, 'Where is the great interviewer?'

'I am here,' he answered, turning around.

'Now, Mr Parkinson, I must tell you, I am somewhat hard of hearing.'

'Well, sir, I do hope that you'll be able to hear my questions.'

'I will be able to hear the ones that I would like to answer,' Madiba replied.

CHAPTER 13

Ear of the nation

ONCE I'D QUALIFIED as a doctor, I tried different specialities, including emergency medicine, cardiology and neurology, but was never sure what I wanted to do. Neurology was my first choice because I thought it might give me some insight into my father's condition. I found it intellectually stimulating and exciting to be able to arrive at a diagnosis, but what then? The discipline hadn't moved on and there wasn't that much you could do to heal the patient. I wanted to be able to 'do', to make a material difference.

Although I settled on ENT, I was never quite happy with it, agonised that I'd made the wrong decision and worried that I'd be stuck with it for life. After completing his medical degree, my brother Richard did an MBA and then went into business. He became remarkably successful and continued to do outstanding work for the community.

I hadn't ever been comfortable with my choice. Even when a major head and neck reconstruction went well, the satisfaction didn't last. There was a restlessness in me that I couldn't override.

That all evaporated the moment I saw Madiba in his chair. As I went through the simple process of cleaning his ears and hearing aids, I could feel myself settling. The niggling doubt was gone. I drove home thinking that if I could help him in a small way, I could live with that. Who would have imagined that removing ear wax could have such a powerful effect?

From that point onwards, I was determined to take care of his batteries, his wax accumulations and the blockage of his hearing aids. His dedicated staff had many things to do, and it was understandable that such small tasks could be overlooked. Zelda was extremely diligent with her care of Madiba, but I wasn't sure who would take full responsibility, on a daily basis, for keeping the hearing aids functional. It worried me that a simple thing such as dysfunctional technology could disable one of the most revered men on earth. Madiba was a good listener, and while he had the ear of the nation – and it could hear him loud and clear – there were times when he could not quite hear the response.

Forgetting that he said he'd only serve for one term, people questioned why he didn't stay on, particularly as the South African constitution allowed for a second term. There were various views. Some said he was simply exhausted. When I asked the question, he told me that in Africa many leaders ruled until they were overthrown or died, and he wanted to set an example and show it was possible to relinquish power with dignity.

There was also the sense that he'd outgrown domestic politics and was ready to walk the world stage. I don't think he anticipated that his successor, Thabo Mbeki, might not want him to play a big international role. But as President Bill Clinton noted, throughout his life Madiba had stayed the course and was determined to die with his boots on.

No one else made this same impact. I saw for myself how something almost magical would happen when Madiba walked into a room. His presence changed the composition of the air people breathed, and, as others have noted, he brought their better selves to the fore. You knew you were in the presence of an extraordinary soul and that these minutes were to be cherished.

In these situations, I watched closely to see if people were aware of his hearing impairment and how they managed it. Many seemed to register it and take it into account. They were more solicitous when they spoke; they wanted to show him respect and be seen to be acknowledged by him. In this regard, his iconic status was largely working in his favour. But a surprising amount of information gets passed casually – information people may not even be conscious of – which helps to build an impression of what's really happening. Every bit missed may have a price. I wondered what price Madiba was paying. Although he was always the centre of attention, were his smile and his gracious demeanour covering gaps?

The legacy of his time in prison was becoming more evident too, and he couldn't get around as easily as before. It was no secret that he had arthritis, and one of his doctors has since revealed that when he was released, he also had cardiomyopathy, which meant his heart was enlarged. There were public reports of his having been hospitalised for tuberculosis, having prostate issues and, much later, having prostate cancer.

But he never let any of this weigh on others, and in all my time with him, he maintained a state of controlled calm. Often, when I go to see patients, they ask or complain about unrelated medical conditions and want advice. Madiba never complained, not even about his ears, and never strayed into his multiple other issues. And I never asked, because I did not want to overstep the boundary. I respected his stoicism. Our meetings usually began and ended with a warm handshake, and I remember how his large hand would envelop mine. It affirmed our contact and made me feel happy.

As Zelda has since written, he was not a difficult person at all. She described him using the beautiful Afrikaans word 'gematig'. There's no exact English equivalent for it, but 'temperate' is close.

Madiba still had a constant stream of friends and interesting visitors coming to the house, and on my way in or out I'd regularly pass old liberation fighters, lawyers who had supported the cause, dignitaries and important overseas guests, some held in high esteem and some less admired. While Madiba had very strong views on certain politicians and moral issues, I never heard him speak badly of people, at least not directly.

CHAPTER 14

Straddling two worlds

THE YEAR 2003 brought the two extremes of my life into sharp focus. While the tranquil sessions with Madiba replenished me, violence beyond his walls depleted me. To keep sane, I used to run with 'Rockies', the Rocky Road Runners. On these runs, we'd wear our fox shirts, bearing the logo of a company that manufactured cleaning cloths.

Early on Saturday morning, 8 October 2003, I got an urgent call to go to that cloth factory owned by my close friend Gerald Fox. I arrived to find him lying on the ground between two small pickup trucks in the parking lot, his lifeless body still warm in a pool of blood. He'd been shot in the back of the head and his staff were standing around motionless with disbelief and grief.

I held Gerald for about three hours as shocked family and friends arrived and police conducted their investigations.

He was still a person to me, not a body. I remembered losing Stephen Pon, and now Gerald was lifeless in my arms. When the police mortuary van arrived and he was taken from me, I got a hosepipe and began washing the blood and secretions off the concrete. An old black man with no teeth, in a G Fox uniform, wanted to assist me. I respectfully said that as he was an old *madala,* a wise elder, I would do the work. He answered that this was his lifelong right and honour. He was the single breadwinner of his clan and only Gerald had offered him a job. He was 80 years old.

I handed over the hosepipe and walked into Gerald's office. On his desk, in his handwriting, was a list of 30 needy families that he had delivered food parcels to the day before, as he had done weekly for years. Each name was carefully written and ticked off. On a prominent place on his desk was a plaque of his famous dictum: 'If I ever get the opportunity to do good, let me not delay, but do it at once, for I may never walk this path again.' Another copy was in the wallet in the pocket of the grey tracksuit pants he was wearing when he was shot.

Gerald was the embodiment of charity. We were in the Rockies running club together, and every week Gerald would collect money from us and others for people in need – orphans, widowers and the like. He only asked once and expected an immediate response. His charity was always anonymous, so as to preserve the pride and dignity of the recipient.

Quite separately, at one point I was approached by an organisation to collect money for 1 000 crutches urgently needed for victims of terror in the Middle East. I needed to raise R110 000 and approached several companies and individuals. When I asked Gerald, his response was predictable: 'With pleasure. Just give me the necessary bank details.' Half an hour later, I received an irate phone call. 'Where are the details already?' he asked. Not five minutes later, I received an SMS from my bank to say that Mr G Fox had deposited R11 000 into the account.

Gerald spoke little, always kept his word and did good deeds across all denominations. For many of us he was a role model, benefactor, friend and confidant. We loved him. Apart from our club, runners all over South Africa had taken to wearing the shirts that Gerald handed out freely. With their fox logo and a declaration that 'we do it cleanly', the shirts had become iconic in the marathon community.

That he was more than just a generous donator of shirts, cleaning rags and caps from his factory was evidenced at his funeral, attended in pouring rain by 3 000 people. Some had to park two kilometres from the cemetery. Night after night, his passing was mourned in the bereavements column of *The Star*.

After Gerald's murder I sank into despair. The next day was my forty-second birthday, but when my family wanted to proceed with the planned celebration, I couldn't face it. I couldn't face anything, nor could I absorb what had happened. I just kept remembering the things Gerald had done. Once he told me he only needed 100 employees, but kept 300 because their age, incompetence or physical disability made them unemployable elsewhere, and they were breadwinners. At the time, I thought he was using a bit of poetic licence.

But about a week after his death, an accountant approached me and asked if he could apologise to me about Gerald Fox. I asked why. His company had conducted an analysis of Gerald's business and had recommended, among other economies, that he reduce his staff from 300 to 125 at most. On hearing this, Gerald asked the analysts to leave. Astonished, the accountant and his colleagues left, deriding Gerald as naive and uncommercial. Now the accountant realised there was more to running a business.

The story of Johnny and Ida, a blind couple with two sighted children, illustrates this. They lived in a small tin shanty in Eldorado Park and until Johnny met Gerald, he survived on handouts and begging. Gerald employed him and his wife and paid the taxi fares to get them to and from work. When he realised the taxis were taking advantage and dropping them at a distance from their shanty, he provided a daily G Fox driver to transport them, door to door.

In the factory, specially designed cloth-cutting machines enabled Johnny and other partially sighted people to operate them safely. In Johnny, Gerald discovered a talented runner, and he sponsored him. Together they ran many Comrades Marathons, hand in hand and linked with a rope. Gerald would navigate them through thousands of runners, spectators and 90 kilometres of hills and road between Durban and Pietermaritzburg.

At the unveiling of Gerald's tombstone, I held Johnny's hand and guided him to the gravesite. He asked me to read out what was inscribed on the tombstone. When I had finished, he said, 'Peter, I understand there is a picture of a fox engraved on the stone.' I confirmed this and he promptly put his hand in his pocket and took out two shining crystals. He said to me, 'Peter, these are my most valuable possessions. Please place each crystal on the eyes of the fox because Gerald was my eyes in this world and the next.'

Some four years later, I gave testimony in court at the sentencing of the men who murdered Gerald. Others declined out of fear that cronies of the convicted men might come after them and their families. I did it out of duty to Gerald.

I never told Madiba about this experience. In those early days of our professional relationship, it seemed inappropriate. He had absorbed so much violence and his personal discipline was so sturdy that it felt cowardly for me to go to pieces over this single act. As time went on, however, the stress of life in a violent South Africa would loosen the barrier between my personal life and my time with Madiba as a professional caregiver.

CHAPTER 15

A common courtesy

THE NOVELTY OF MEETING Madiba never wore off for me. I always made sure that I was well dressed, that my kit was in order and that I had read the morning newspapers. Most importantly, I made sure that I was early. More than once, he told me that he regarded time as precious and that it was a common courtesy to show others respect by being on time. This echoed a maxim from my childhood. My mother would regularly remind us that 'punctuality is the politeness of princes'. We didn't understand what this meant, but we knew we had to be punctual.

For Madiba you needed more than punctuality. You needed to be early because you couldn't risk the smallest margin of lateness. If you weren't on time, there was a high chance he wouldn't see you. He had lost so much time in jail, he didn't know how much he had left, and every minute was important. He also followed a strict routine. Over the years I got to know this routine.

Occasionally, I'd be asked to come to the house early, before he went down the road to the offices of the Nelson Mandela Foundation, or to come to the Foundation itself. It had been established to provide infrastructure for him when his presidential term ended, and it managed his diary while taking care of his public life. The foundation was there to protect his legacy and, as he grew frail, to relieve the load on him and represent him to the world.

Often, I was asked to arrive at Madiba's home at 11 am, by which time he had read three English daily newspapers and one in Afrikaans. Another Afrikaans paper was delivered in the afternoon. As he completed each paper, he made sure all the pages were aligned before folding them so precisely that it looked as if the paper had not been read. He respected these sources of news and, from the time of his release, had used them to navigate his way through the new world, identifying people and organisations that might help in the process of transforming the country.

He would read about a person and then ask for a meeting. Newspapers also held memories from his time in prison. In the very early years, he and other prisoners occasionally found pieces of old newspapers on the garbage heap on Robben Island and would consume them with great interest. It was only after 17 years of incarceration that they were formally permitted to read the papers, in 1980.

He always read the Afrikaans paper first and when I asked about this, he said he had taught himself the language on the island. Why? Because when you negotiate with your enemy, if you don't speak his language you're already at a disadvantage. 'When you speak his language, you can enter his heart, not only his mind,' he said. He became fluent and was able to negotiate on behalf of all the other prisoners on the island, and gain concessions on clothing, sunglasses and working hours. These wins made a significant daily difference to prisoners, and he was convinced they were only achieved because he spoke the warders' language.

In my last years with him, our relationship was more relaxed and he spoke a lot about the warders – how hard they were on him, how they initially hated him and how he gradually won them over. He did this by talking to them about their interests and treating them with respect, in their own tongue. Eventually, he said, they became friends. Genuine good friends.

I usually knew when Madiba wanted to say something important about an issue or a person. He would tell me a story from which I had to divine the lesson. These teachings always began with the phrase 'No, doctor …' and I was always warm for them. Sitting with him in his living room, I could sense that lost tradition of older men imparting wisdom to the younger men at their feet. His unusual use of the word 'no' to start a sentence was not a negative; it was a polite pause, a chance to collect his thoughts.

While Madiba was always respectful and punctual, he felt no need to be polite if people disrespected his time and were late, even if they were very important figures. This was underlined by an episode I saw on television after he stood down from office in June 1999.

Thabo Mbeki was elected as the second black president of South Africa and both he and Madiba were due to speak at a televised state function. Madiba had known Thabo's father, Govan Mbeki. During the struggle, they'd spent long years in jail together. Thabo was the new generation, an intellectual in a Savile Row suit.

The night of the dinner there was a delay and Thabo arrived late. When it was Madiba's turn to speak, he stood up and publicly rebuked the younger man for his lack of punctuality. It was an awkward moment, but he had the authority, the age and the courage do this without a qualm.

In fact, there are numerous stories about Madiba's refusal to tolerate 'African time'. One morning, I arrived just as he had finished reading the papers that headlined yet another atrocity committed by President Robert Mugabe of Zimbabwe. So I asked him what he thought of Mugabe. He responded not with criticism but with a kind of parable. By this time, invasions of white farms, which had begun in 2000, were rampant. Appalled by this, Mandela had called Mugabe a tyrant. The relationship between the two men was not warm.

He turned to me and, as he began with 'No, doctor ...', I settled back in my chair. He related an incident that had taken place on a steel railway bridge over the Zambezi River. Situated just beyond the spectacular Victoria Falls, this bridge joins Zimbabwe and Zambia and has historic significance. It was the brainchild of the colonialist and empire builder Cecil John Rhodes, who dreamed of seeing Africa connected, from Cape to Cairo, with a continuous railway. His dream was never realised but the bridge was opened in 1905 by Charles Darwin's son. Seventy years later, major peace talks took place halfway across the bridge in a South African Railways train. The aim was to reach a settlement in troubled Rhodesia (now Zimbabwe). The discussion between a delegation from the incumbent white government of Rhodesia and a delegation comprising three black parties was mediated by the South African prime minister and the Zambian president. It didn't work. The talks broke down the same day, no settlement was reached, and the undertaking was regarded as unsuccessful. The same would happen with a meeting between Madiba and Mugabe at the same spot in July 2001.

Madiba was in Zambia for a summit of the Organisation of African Unity when he received a request for a meeting from Mugabe. He agreed and it was arranged that they would meet at the midway point of the bridge at 12 noon. As was his way, Madiba arrived 15 minutes early and walked along the path beside the train track for 100 metres to the centre of the bridge. There was no Mugabe.

He remained there until the appointed time, and then a little longer. Astonished that Mugabe could be late, he retraced his steps and waited on the Zambian side. Mugabe arrived an hour and a half late. Both men then walked to the midpoint. When Mugabe put out his hand in a greeting, Madiba took off his wristwatch (he showed me how he took it off) and, rather than shaking hands, handed it to Mugabe saying, 'President Mugabe, here is a gift, because either you don't have one of these or yours doesn't function.'

'And with that, doctor, I turned around, and I've never spoken to or seen him again,' he said. Mugabe felt the full weight of that iron fist beneath the velvet glove, and would later attempt to land a few blows himself.

Madiba radically shifted the long-standing dynamic between the two men. This was not an impulsive move: he was determined to remain loyal to those leaders who had supported the ANC during the long years of apartheid and Mugabe had been exemplary in this regard. Among other things, he had given sanctuary to liberation fighters. But Madiba's antipathy to Mugabe had been building for years, and this was a considered closing of the relationship. Madiba was the great conciliator of the era, although in this case, no conciliation ever followed.

The relationship had started out well. Just 16 days after his release, Madiba took a trip around southern Africa to demonstrate his gratitude. First stop was Lusaka, the capital of Zambia, which had served as headquarters for the ANC since the 1970s. He received a welcome fit for a head of state, with President Kenneth Kaunda and other notables waiting for him on the runway.

Then it was on to Zimbabwe, where his plane was met by drummers and dancers on the tarmac. He descended the stairs into Mugabe's embrace. True to his word, Madiba remained loyal to Mugabe for a decade. He and other South African leaders rarely criticised Mugabe, believing that quiet diplomacy was the best way to manage the deteriorating situation in Zimbabwe. But eventually Madiba changed position and called for Mugabe to leave office because of the way he was running the country. He famously quipped that Mugabe had been a star, but then the sun came out.

The two men had lived parallel lives in adjoining countries. They were both born in an era of white supremacy; they both went to Christian mission schools and then to the same university, Fort Hare. Each advocated violence against the white regime in their country and each served long prison sentences. But that's where the similarities ended. When Mugabe came to power, he used force to assert majority rule and was internationally reviled. Madiba used dialogue and was celebrated.

Relations between them remained strained, with Mugabe describing Madiba as 'too much of a saint', who had left the South African whites with too much power. 'Mandela has gone a bit too far in doing good to the non-black communities, really in some cases at the expense of [black people],' Mugabe was famously quoted as saying in the *Sunday Independent* newspaper.

When I asked Madiba how he felt about this, he smiled and said he welcomed the criticism because it helped to destroy the myth that he was an angel and was beyond reproach. He didn't want to be heaped with praise and perceived as perfect. I could see that being continually lauded could be exhausting. People often heard him repeat the trope that he'd made many mistakes in his life and was just a sinner, trying to do better. He said this to me several times.

Many years later, when Madiba passed away, Mugabe was slow to offer condolences. When he did, he said Comrade Mandela had been a 'great friend' and that it was not true that they hadn't got along, as had been suggested by the media.

Mugabe was not the first African leader to feel the edge of Madiba's blade. In 1995, when writer Ken Saro-Wiwa and other activists in Nigeria were executed by the military government, Madiba declared it a heinous act that ignored appeals by the world community for a delay in the court order. International pressure had saved Madiba himself from the death penalty and allowed him a life sentence instead. In sentencing, life doesn't necessarily mean lifelong, and here he was, working for change. He warned that South Africa would recommend the expulsion of Nigeria from the Commonwealth pending the installation of a democratic government.

Similarly, Mugabe was not the sole critic of Madiba on the international stage. Many disapproved of the way he engaged as freely with dictatorships as he did with liberal democracies. The Western press could not wrap their heads around this and went on and on about it. How could he see the president of Cuba one day and the president of the US the next? How could anyone be so completely non-partisan? Geopolitics is about allies with shared values, and for this a politician needs to have a clear position. But, at this stage of his life, Madiba was a statesman, not a politician.

And he wasn't a traditional Western statesman either. He wasn't going to abandon those who had supported the black struggle in South Africa. While so many Western democracies had thrown their support behind apartheid and had benefited roundly from the relationship, many dictatorships had quietly and steadfastly backed the push for equality in South Africa, even if things were not quite equal in their own backyard. And after Madiba's release, when the ANC needed funding to prepare for the coming election, it has been reported that funding was made available from dictatorships such as Libya. But dig deep enough and there are contradictions in every position. In the 1960s, when Madiba was on trial, much of the international pressure for him to be spared the death sentence came from Western governments.

While the lines of allegiance were not entirely clear, Madiba found his way forward. 'Our moral authority dictates that we should not abandon those who helped us in the darkest hour in the history of this country. Not only did they support us in rhetoric, they also gave us the resources for us to conduct the struggle,' he famously said. While I loved sitting in his lounge listening to his stories and hearing his views, I never felt it was my place to debate his decisions.

In his post-presidential years, I was often called to the house at the last minute to clean his ears ahead of an important face-to-face meeting or a teleconference. While his visits to my rooms would be formal affairs, carefully arranged by the Foundation with precise timing, a convoy, a security detail and assistants, and while my visits to the house were sometimes diarised in advance, there were many informal requests. I always made a plan and attended. Madiba would hear the words of many leaders, but there is a difference between hearing and listening – you hear with your ears, but you interpret and listen with your brain. My sole task was to make sure he could hear clearly enough, so that he could listen without strain. There were numerous occasions when a call would come while I was in the room. With that, I would stand and excuse myself.

While he was becoming more selective about the international work he did, he gave me the clear impression that his successor, President Mbeki, felt somewhat eclipsed by this and didn't appreciate his role as a global negotiator. He told me Mbeki regarded him as an old man who should retire. As he had already retired, it would be a matter of retiring from retirement. I didn't see it at the time, but in retrospect I think Mbeki initiated the erosion of Madiba's legacy within South Africa. There had been international criticism but cutting him down at home was different.

One morning, I was sitting in Madiba's study refitting his hearing aids when the phone rang. As I was closest, he asked me to answer it. A voice told me that Russian president Vladimir Putin was waiting on the line. Yeah, right. I was about to replace the receiver when I suddenly remembered where I was. Putin could well be on the line, and, in fact, he was. I handed over the receiver and left the room.

As I waited to complete my task, I remembered seeing photos of Madiba and President Boris Yeltsin in Moscow. Both their presidencies were coming to an end, and at the time, Madiba regretted not having made Russia one of the first countries he visited. He said the Soviet Union gave 'enormous assistance' to the ANC's struggle, and he should have acknowledged that debt much earlier.

Madiba's Western critics shook their heads at his relationships with figures such as Fidel Castro, Muammar Gaddafi and Syrian dictator Hafez al-Assad, but all these men had offered unwavering support to the ANC during the decades when great Western democracies were propping up the South African regime. When these democracies finally switched sides and began supporting change in South Africa, they expected that the new ANC government would automatically pivot, fall in behind them and eschew the leaders of places such as Cuba.

On his travels, Madiba's moral authority enabled him to buzz from one president to another, without regard to the ideological distance between them. When he visited Castro, and then immediately flew north to visit Bush Senior, the US media found this unacceptable. But then Madiba could straddle apparent opposites. I believe he knew there would be a political clash but chose not to be derailed by it because he thought about the world differently.

One afternoon, he told me the story of Bush sitting him down in the Oval Office and offering him Kentucky bourbon. Madiba declined. When asked if there was anything else he'd prefer, he cheerfully answered, 'Yes, please, I'll have some Cuban rum.'

CHAPTER 16

Hello, I'm Nelson

O NE MORNING, WE GOT WORD that Madiba would be arriving in my consulting rooms at 11 am. It was 9 am. We had two hours to reschedule everyone and clear the rooms. The police arrived early and all the exits and entries to Milpark Hospital were cleared. Of course, wherever Madiba went, there was great excitement. In seconds the news was flying through the hospital corridors. Everyone knew about his imminent arrival and the precise route he would take through the labyrinth.

As 11 am approached, people poured out of wards, operating theatres, laboratories, kitchens, offices and cleaning stations, and began to line the wide passages of the new part of the hospital. I waited at the entrance and watched as Madiba got out of the car and, much to the chagrin of his security detail, began to greet as many people as he could. Typically, he stepped up, shook hands, and said, 'Hello, I'm

Nelson.' Many had never seen him in the flesh and were so affected by his forcefield that they couldn't respond. His energy was palpable. Then, as he walked down the main thoroughfare, holding my hand, some of the staff began ululating, others were clapping, and most were tearful. As we approached the oldest part of the hospital the corridors narrowed, but still there were people lining them.

When we turned into my rooms, he strode directly up to the two women at the reception desk. 'Hello, ladies. I wonder if you can help me, please. My name is Nelson. I'm an old man, but I'm looking for a job. Would you perhaps have one for me?' He shook their hands and told them they were lucky to be working with such a young doctor and that the work they were doing was very important: 'And I want you to know that I appreciate it.'

Then he asked to meet the person who cleans my rooms. Angela (Angie) Mafefane stepped forward. He shook her hand and they spoke in isiXhosa. Later, Angie translated their exchange to me. 'You don't know me, but my family knows you,' she said. Madiba asked for her surname and, without pausing, happily confirmed he knew her parents and her grandmothers, but he'd not known her because he was in prison while she was growing up.

Angie had spent her childhood playing with his daughters in the streets of Orlando West, in Soweto, by then a large black city on the edge of Johannesburg. She lived at 8122 Vilakazi Street, just a few houses away from his girls and their mother, Winnie, at number 8115. She called Winnie 'aunty' because she always cooked for the street, gave the children clothes and took them to school. Her parents had told her that Madiba had been the lawyer for all the locals, including themselves, and was legendary for charging affordable fees, usually 45 cents a consultation.

Later, Angie explained that she'd been overcome by the meeting and had rushed home to share the experience, but her family and parents didn't believe her. How could a cleaner be so close to the president (they still called him president) and actually speak to him? When she produced a photograph taken in the room, they were speechless.

Meantime, Shamim and I were nervous. Shamim had never seen Madiba before and was overwhelmed all over again. But she managed to contain herself and took him into the hearing booth, set him up and explained the procedure. Then she fitted him with earphones and a bone conductor behind each ear. As we tested his hearing, we were shocked at how poor it was.

Then we tested the benefit he was getting from his hearing aids, and it was not much at all. Shamim and I agreed that it didn't feel right to do any more there and then. So she just adjusted his existing hearing aids to optimise them. Madiba was delighted. The whole exercise took about 30 minutes, and he was on his way. We had our evidence and showed Mike the results. Seeing the report, he agreed Madiba would benefit from state-of-art digital hearing aids that could be programmed for one's specific pattern of hearing loss.

One of the problems is that, initially, many people don't like the new sophisticated devices and believe they are not working properly because they aren't loud and don't blast environmental noise. It takes the brain six to eight weeks to adjust and, when it does, their understanding of speech greatly improves. When I explained all this to Madiba, saying he would certainly benefit from these new devices, I didn't anticipate his response. The discussion became difficult:

'No, doctor, I'm not losing these hearing aids,' he said emphatically, pointing to the ones in his ears.

'But they are very old. Think of the car you drove before you went to prison and compare it to the beautiful BMW you have today. Like cars, hearing aids have changed too.'

'No, doctor, that's not the point. These hearing aids were donated to me when I came out of prison, and I don't want to seem ungrateful to the people who gave them to me. I do not want them to be affected. And so, doctor, I'm going to stick with them. My answer is no.'

I took a deep breath and pushed on. 'Madiba, many world leaders wear hearing aids today, but none of them are wearing the ones you have. I know you are a close friend of President Bill Clinton. He has hearing loss from playing the saxophone, using hunting rifles and being at too many political rallies with booming music. Since 1997, he's been wearing hearing aids in both ears.'

'No, doctor, I did not see him wearing hearing aids.'

'That's because they fit deep in his ear; they are called ITC, for in-the-canal hearing aids. We can get those for you. We can ask the company that provided your hearing aids, or we can go to another company.'

After a few more rounds, I won him over. 'Okay, doctor. You have made a persuasive argument. I will listen to you.'

I was thrilled Madiba had agreed to update his hearing devices and arranged for a company to donate a state-of-the-art pair of hearing aids. They were very expensive and had tiny moulds that could hardly be seen inside the ear. Shamim came with me to the house to fit them and we were beaming as we carried our prize inside.

We had difficulty getting them into his ears but we managed. 'No, doctor, it is no use, they are not working,' he said, immediately wanting his old ones back. I explained that it takes time to get used to the sound and that he needed to come to the rooms where we had the equipment and software to program them.

In the rooms, we completed the programming and when we again played him the test tape, he began hearing sounds he hadn't heard for years. Birds were chirping again, some musical notes that had vanished were back, and a few consonants that had disappeared reappeared. He walked into the reception area and, for the first time, heard the noise of the computers at work. Then a bell rang, and he heard it. He broke into a wide smile as he turned to the noise, and we realised he'd heard it. It moved us almost to tears and we looked at each other, thinking what a wonderful thing we'd done.

But when we asked him to remove the devices, he fumbled. He just couldn't get the tiny things out. From years of chipping away at the limestone on Robben Island, his hands were arthritic and his fingers too swollen to manipulate the moulds. In that moment I realised how arrogant I'd been. We thought we could provide this exceptional human being with the smallest possible moulds, so that, like other world leaders, no one would see he was wearing them. But he couldn't put them in and he couldn't take them out. Rather than helping him, they'd only make him more dependent.

I removed the devices and said, 'Madiba, I want to

apologise sincerely, because I have made a mistake. We made very small moulds so no one would see them.'

He looked at me and said, 'No, doctor, you see, I don't care if people see that I wear hearing aids; it's good that they know I have a problem and that I'm doing something about it.'

'Madiba, I'll use the same technology but have big moulds made for you.'

'Yes, doctor, that's very good. You will make me what I need.' As always, he spoke very simply, with depth and no blame.

That week, we had big brown moulds made that were plain to see. He was thoroughly delighted with them as they sat comfortably in his ears, and he could put them in and remove them without effort.

But I knew they wouldn't be optimal in a press conference or around a table with many voices interacting from different directions. So we organised a remote frequency-modulated system that picked up the sound in the room, or on people's microphones, and transmitted it directly to his hearing aids. Madiba's minders needed to put the device on the table, and make sure he was wearing a hearing loop around his neck and that it was tuned into the device's Wi-Fi and switched on.

When he tried it the first time, he described the loop system as incredible. He couldn't believe that he could sit with a large group and when someone in the corner spoke, even if it was unclear or in a different accent, it was picked up by his monitor on the table and went straight to his hearing aid. While he always expressed his gratitude, our biggest problem was persuading his managers to bring the monitor to meetings and to turn it on. Often, they just didn't get around to it.

Hearing loss can be exhausting. Not only is there the social strain of asking people to repeat themselves, there is mental fatigue from the brain working overtime trying to make sense of the fragments it receives. As hearing loss is often invisible and the burden of it can't be seen either, it's easy for others to minimise its impact.

The way Madiba's hearing loss was relegated to a secondary concern was frustrating, and my efforts to give it more prominence often created tension. Although I'd been going to the house for a few years, some still regarded me as an annoying newcomer who wanted to change things. I was always trying to explain that just because Madiba didn't ask for help, it didn't mean he didn't need it.

By openly acknowledging his hearing loss, he was in good company. John Howard, Australia's second-longest-serving prime minister, had long worn hearing aids, and despite hearing loss leading to a slight speech impediment, he credited some of his political success to his hearing impairment. It necessitated a reliance on memory and led him to develop an assertive speaking voice to compensate for the lack of hearing.

Over time, Madiba's speech patterns changed too. A recording of his speech from the dock in 1964 has him speaking fluently, with normal cadence and speed. For rhetorical effect, he deliberately pauses between sentences. He was in his mid-forties, and I expected that back then his hearing was intact.

By the time of his release in 1990, his 71-year-old voice was still strong but had slowed. Even with allowances for rhetoric, he paused more often between phrases.

In his post-presidential years, as he moved deeper into his eighties, occasionally he paused between words. This often happens to people who lose their hearing; they speak slowly so they can hear their own voice, and they pause to ensure others have heard it too.

While Madiba was in jail, in 1983, Ronald Reagan became the first US president to wear hearing aids while in office. His hearing loss had begun during his acting career half a century earlier when a gun was fired very close to his right ear. His willingness to wear small new devices reduced stigma and boosted the hearing-aid industry in the country.

CHAPTER 17

Your enemy is
not necessarily my enemy

OUTSIDE OF MY MEDICAL expertise, I never contested anything Madiba said. I didn't have the confidence, and when it came to international affairs, I generally didn't have the knowledge. But I was very interested in the Middle East and particularly in his line of argument on the Palestinian cause. His antipathy to the occupation of East Jerusalem and the West Bank of the Jordan River, which Israel took over in the 1967, was well known. This was heatedly discussed in the South African Jewish and Islamic communities, and when there was a news item about it, I would often raise the subject.

He knew I was Jewish, and before such a discussion began, he would look at me and say, 'Remember, your enemy is not necessarily my enemy.' During the long years of apartheid, while Israel supported South Africa, at least with arms, the Palestine Liberation Organization (PLO) supported the struggle against apartheid. For the PLO, Madiba was regarded as a fellow freedom fighter in the global family of liberation movements. In turn, Madiba described the PLO's leader, Yasser Arafat, as 'a comrade in arms'.

Following Madiba's release from jail, Arafat was one of the first men he saw on his initial trip out of South Africa. By the end of 1994, both these men had become presidents: Madiba of South Africa and Arafat of the Palestinian National Authority, and both had won a Nobel Peace Prize. There were many views of Arafat. For Palestinians, he was a freedom fighter; for Israelis, he was a terrorist. Some commentators criticised Arafat for being too willing to make concessions to the Israelis, while others suggested he might be corrupt. Madiba supported him regardless.

One afternoon, I was attending to Madiba's ears ahead of a possible phone meeting with Arafat on one line and Israeli prime minister Ariel Sharon on another. When the phone rang, I left the room, as was required. How I would have loved to stay! Imagine eavesdropping on such an exchange. But then, I was not sure who was actually on the phone and what transpired. There was, however, hope in my heart: if there was a single person in the world who had the capacity, the authority and the trust to achieve a solution in the Middle East, it was Madiba. He would fight for the rights of both sides. Publicly, and in our discussions, he had repeated that the occupation needed to end, but for this to happen, Israel's right to exist had to be acknowledged too.

Madiba could not be gagged. He could say whatever he wanted, and he did. Some local politicians and world leaders who couldn't reach his heights were envious of his stature and frustrated at being overshadowed. I saw evidence of this directly when, on another visit, the phone rang. I waited outside. It didn't take long.

When I returned, Madiba was visibly irked. There was an important piece of negotiation he wanted to initiate between the Palestinians and the Israelis, but President Mbeki had cut him out. 'He wants the "old man" to mind his own business,' Madiba said, without expounding further. But more than once, he had told me that when it came to the world stage, Mbeki and some other world leaders regarded him as meddling and troublesome.

What a pity. His reputation for impartiality should have made him acceptable to all sides. This troubled me and I wondered if his age and his hearing loss had something to do with the loss of regard by some leaders. While he retained his international standing, he no longer had the same level of engagement. Was it only age or was his hearing impairment silently accelerating the isolation? I was always on the lookout for unrecognised features of his hearing loss. For us, an improvement of one or two per cent was significant.

When Arafat died in 2004, Madiba described him as an icon and one of the outstanding freedom fighters of his generation. He also expressed his sadness that Arafat's dream of a Palestinian state had not been realised. He noted that when he, Madiba, was released from jail, he rapidly received invitations from almost every country in the world, but the one from Israel didn't arrive for some time.

Yet, behind these discussions, I knew he had high regard for many members of South Africa's Jewish community.

In his difficult early days in Johannesburg, they helped in different ways, not least giving him a job as a lawyer, hiding him as a fugitive, being part of his legal team and representing him in court. But then the prosecutor in the trial that sent him to jail for life had also been Jewish.

Madiba could separate people from their politics and did exactly this with the Jewish people he encountered in South Africa and the politics of Israel. Quite plainly, he said he owed a debt of honour to the Jews, even if he made critical remarks about Israel. He believed that both the Jewish people and the Palestinian people had a right to their own states and said he would fight for both of them. In the same manner he fought against both white and black domination in South Africa, so he explained he would always fight against both Israeli and Palestinian domination in the Middle East.

But his words were regularly misinterpreted or misquoted to suit different agendas. In a speech on 4 December 1997 for the International Day of Solidarity with the Palestinian People, in Pretoria, Madiba stated, 'But we know too well that our freedom is incomplete without the freedom of the Palestinians; without the resolution of conflicts in East Timor, the Sudan and other parts of the world.'

In the 1980s, he had twice refused a conditional early release from jail, stating that only a completely free man can negotiate. He never wavered from that position and applied it to the Palestinian people. They too needed their unconditional freedom before entering negotiations. This left many on the Jewish and Israeli sides uncomfortable.

Opposed to Israel's control of the territories it had 'occupied' in the Six-Day War, for the sake of peace Madiba urged it to concede land to the Palestinians and Syrians, just as it had done with the Egyptians. On his first visit to Israel in December 1999, his interview with journalists was recorded by Israel Radio English news, and later reported in *The Jerusalem Post* by Steve Linde in December 2013: 'I understand completely well why Israel occupies these lands. There was a war. But if there is going to be peace, there must be complete withdrawal from all of these areas.' He did, however, continue to acknowledge Israel's legitimate security concerns, saying, 'I cannot conceive of Israel withdrawing if Arab states do not recognise Israel within secure borders.'

I respected him even more for this. In 1999, he visited Israel for the first time and faced several difficult questions about the reasons for his trip. As usual, his answers were direct:

'Israel worked very closely with the apartheid regime. I say: I've made peace with many men who slaughtered our own people like animals. Israel cooperated with the apart-heid regime, but it did not participate in any atrocities.'

Madiba had explained this several times to me before. Here was a key tenet of his negotiation strategy: you cannot expect to negotiate and make peace with angels on either side. Both parties 'slaughtered' their enemies, but to make peace, you have to be practical. You are entitled never to forget but you must forgive to move forward.

In front of his chair in the lounge, where he liked to sit, he had a Quran, an Old Testament and the New Testament, all bound in silver. There may have been other texts, I can't remember, but I do know he was a universalist and could see beyond the boundaries of nationalism, tribalism and religion.

I left this visit troubled and frustrated. Sometimes, during a sleepless night, I used to revisit Madiba in his chair and replay his talking about this ailing patch of land. Had he been released earlier, he might have had more time for this issue and possibly might have helped it to heal.

CHAPTER 18

How much to disclose?

T HE MORE I WENT to Madiba's house, the easier and the more complicated my relationship with the household became. While my visits with Shamim were almost always formally scheduled, many of my visits alone were spontaneous. If something unexpected arose, I could be called to the house at short notice. It was not unusual for Madiba's family and his physician to ring me without notifying those who kept his diary at the Foundation. The security guards knew me and happily waved me in. The kitchen staff were accustomed to my wandering in through the back door and would stop for a chat. But I was making demands on the house staff about the hearing issue, and these were unwelcome. I was conscious never to raise this in front of Madiba or Graça.

In retrospect, I was probably a bit pushy, wanting my narrow area of interest to have primacy. The staff had lots to do, and caring for his hearing was an added burden. Over time, I would find that his batteries were flat or that supplies had run out or that his hearing aids were clogged.

Madiba had lived through much violence, directly and vicariously. He'd experienced it personally, he'd seen it committed on others and, perhaps worst of all, when in prison he had read about and been informed about it being meted out to his then wife, Winnie. Helpless to protect her, all he had been able to do was encourage her to build internal fortifications against it.

So, when violence found its way into my life, I was never sure about whether I should mention it. It was not a topic we generally discussed, and I decided I wouldn't tell him about the bread-and-butter stuff, just about those incidents that shook me so severely that they rearranged my priorities. When, in the sanctuary of his house, I did relate such events, he would look at me as I spoke, listen to every word, hear every pause and remain silent, leaving quiet understanding between us.

While the threat of violence was ever present in our part of Johannesburg, our life wasn't grim. Everyone in our community lived with it, and because of it we became closer. We watched out for each other, looked after each other, shared intelligence and if something bad happened we all offered support. If there was something to celebrate, we gave it our best. There was a lot of joy. Of course there were tensions from time to time, but overall it was an emotionally rich period, with a lot of cooperation and children moving between houses. I knew that if we left the country, our family would never live with such intensity again, nor find ourselves another community that would be as familiar and as comfortable.

Linda was enjoying a successful career. Known as Dr Linda, she had a television programme, appeared on talk shows, had a magazine column, was frequently in the newspaper, had written books and was recognised wherever she went. She also ran a medical practice for women. If we left, what would become of all this? It was rooted in South Africa and wasn't transportable. Her work did, however, have an international dimension and she used to travel to the UK, Europe and the US as a keynote speaker at conferences and on the corporate circuit. This, we thought, might not be affected. My prospects were not bright either. I could always find work to feed the family, but beyond that I didn't really know how well I'd translate overseas. At least, if we went, we'd be liberated from fear.

For example, we wouldn't have to worry about a simple thing like getting the children to school safely. As the little public transport that functioned was no longer safe, we had lift schemes to drop and collect them. In our suburb, having children wait on the pavement was out of the question. The car had to come through the gates, and when they closed again, the children climbed in or out. But the security gates were a point of vulnerability because, although mechanised, they were slow. People could slip in or a driver with bad intentions could jam them open before they closed.

One afternoon at around 3:30 pm, as our children were being dropped off, two well-dressed men brandishing weapons followed the car though the gate. Linda dashed to the car. As the men shouted and pulled out the terrified driver, Linda somehow got all the children into the house, and left the front door ajar so the driver could find refuge too. Fortunately, the men were only interested in the car and drove off. Linda had not buzzed the gates closed. Trapping the men on the property could have been catastrophic.

This incident might not sound like much, but it was one of many and the cumulative effect destabilised the children. Without going into too much detail, one morning our neighbour was shot in the upper abdomen while answering a knock on her front door. Linda, who was a GP, went to her aid and called for help. It looked like a bullet had hit her liver and Linda stayed with her until a trauma helicopter set down on a nearby field. Then, a few months later, Linda's parents were hijacked in our driveway. The gunman was not a good shot and missed. The children heard it all.

While others had suffered far more severely, and people everywhere were affected, I could find no peace. I was tipped over the edge one Sunday afternoon when I tried, against the odds, to save a baby who had been shot while sitting on her mother's lap in a stationary car. I couldn't resuscitate the child; the mother was hysterical and there was nothing I could do.

I began planning to take my family out of the country and registered with the British and Irish medical councils. I also began looking for opportunities in Australia. Linda was reluctant to move. She said we should use our skills in South Africa, where they were most needed. As it was proving hard to find a job in Sydney or Melbourne, I shelved the idea. Linda was correct, of course, but I continued to fret about the safety of our young family.

I'm reluctant to go on and on about the suburban violence, but there was more to come for us. A year or so later, our young twin daughters were held up in a local hairdressing salon. They were waiting for haircuts and had nothing of value to give the gunmen. Fortunately, others had cash, mobile phones and jewellery to surrender. It wasn't long after that incident that, on a Saturday afternoon, I was walking home with two of my sons when a hijacking unfolded before our eyes. The boys and I hid crouching behind bushes until the car disappeared. Its trembling owner was spared.

In the school playground, the children swapped horror stories, and in class they were given instructions on how to conduct themselves during a hijacking. Who should they listen to – their parents or the men (and they were mostly men) with guns? By then, it was not unusual for our children to drag their mattresses into our bedroom at night. I was also saying a prayer every morning as I reversed out of my garage.

Those prayers were answered one night, about six months after I bought a new BMW 3 series. Linda and I were on the way home when I noticed we were being shadowed by a large black BMW X5 SUV. It stayed close and its lack of number plates left us in no doubt about what was happening. I took an odd turn; it followed. I took another and it did the same. We had an armed guard outside our house and as I came down our street, with the silhouette of the predator behind me, the guard took one look and disappeared into the small gatehouse.

I told Linda to get on the floor, and outside our house I started hooting madly and flashing the lights, causing as much commotion as possible. I'd stopped in the middle of the road, thinking that if the hijackers came up in front of me, I could reverse, and if they got out of the car I could speed off. But they drove up alongside with their guns, looked down into our car and then, miraculously, took off.

The next morning, I went to the BMW dealer to hand in the keys. The dealer offered me 70 per cent of the purchase price. When I took it, he couldn't believe his luck. Then I got a small white Lexus. Why? Because in those days, I was told, Lexus was not available elsewhere on the continent. This meant there was no point hijacking it, because in South Africa imported cars were stolen and taken directly to chop shops. The parts were then sent along illegal market routes into the rest of Africa.

By mid-2005, I had managed to reduce my trauma exposure at work. I was appointed the clinical head of the ENT Academic Department at Wits University Donald Gordon Medical Centre in Parktown, which did not have a level-one emergency unit. However, violent robberies and hijackings were happening almost daily in our larger neighbourhood. It was nerve-wracking, and I was extremely fearful for my family. I jumped at unexpected noises and couldn't sleep. Eventually, I made a pact with myself: the only way I could justify staying in South Africa was if I could genuinely protect my family. I would have to do everything in my power to make our environment secure. But what to do?

Many of us were already subscribers to an 'instant armed response' service and we displayed their signage outside our homes. When called, one or perhaps two security guards would arrive in a small SUV. But this was usually after the fact, and they would be too late. Although these services were a deterrent, they were inadequate.

We also experimented with a neighbourhood watch for the suburbs of Savoy and Waverley. In pairs, people would drive around, and if they noticed anything they would alert the residents. But these 'watchers' were unarmed and of little use in an incident. They could and they did call the overstretched and under-resourced police, who would arrive sometime later.

Following several crime-related tragedies in the nearby suburb of Glenhazel, experts were commissioned to design a mechanism to combat crime in the community. In 2006, Glenhazel Active Protection (GAP) was launched. Knowing that we had similar problems in our neighbourhood, we were approached and encouraged to adopt the same scheme.

This was an ambitious, labour-intensive scheme. To implement it, we needed to raise a staggering R6 million. Two of us took charge of setting it up. Alan Greenstein, a banker, and I spared no effort in making it work. This was our last stand; if it proved successful, we could remain in South Africa. Success meant creating a safe precinct for all residents of Waverley and Savoy, including of course, the children.

We had to rent premises for a control centre, buy heavy SUVs, employ trained armed guards and have the best available communication system. The guards would drive around and be on call 24/7. This would be a small legal paramilitary force. Using the Glenhazel template, we sought approval from local municipal wards, regional councils, the police, institutions, schools and businesses of the area. The task took six months to accomplish. When we knocked on the doors of most of the houses too, the answer was a resounding yes. People wanted it.

In my small street alone, I visited all 12 houses to find each had experienced at least one home invasion. But as neighbourhood life had changed, and everyone had high walls, didn't walk in the street and didn't communicate with one another, most thought their incident had been an isolated one. When the headmistress of St Mary's School gave us the use of the school hall, we called a community meeting and 900 people turned up. When it was my turn to speak, I asked for a show of hands: 'How many of you have never experienced a violent crime in your home or in the street, or never witnessed one in the neighbourhood or don't have someone close who has experienced one?' Two people raised their hands.

We needed funding to create the infrastructure, and monthly subscriptions from households to keep it running and ensure financial stability. By then it was called CAP (Community Active Protection) and subscribers displayed CAP signs on their houses warning intruders that the house was protected. Non-subscribers got protection without paying. There were teething problems, but the system succeeded in dramatically reducing crime.

From those early beginnings, CAP now operates in several areas of Johannesburg and offers a range of additional security services, from guards to armed escorts to cleanups and intelligence analysis. It claims it reduces crime on average by 80 to 90 per cent across its communities. Knowing CAP was awake allowed me to sleep. But that comfort was short-lived.

In a couple of years, one of my friends would be fatally shot a few hundred metres outside our arbitrary CAP boundary. That would make me rethink everything.

CHAPTER 19

For him they clapped, but for Zuma they ululated

O N A SWELTERING DAY in January 2006, I was early
for my appointment with Madiba, so I pulled into
a petrol station around the corner from his house.
This is where I regularly filled up and I thought I'd get a
cold drink and kill fifteen minutes while my car was being
washed. Something unusual was going on: people were in
high spirits and there was a buzz in the air. When I asked,
everyone was keen to share the news. Jacob Zuma's convoy
had just passed through and, unbelievably, the man himself
had been in his car as it was being filled.

Demonstrating their respect and affection, they referred
to Zuma by his clan's name, Msholozi, and behaved as if the
Messiah had just stopped by. 'He's our father, he's our leader,
he's our next president,' an exuberant attendant explained
to me. I was taken aback. This didn't reflect what I thought

was the common wisdom about Zuma, and certainly didn't match what I'd gleaned in the white press. It held that Zuma had fallen from grace and was all but written off. As a political force, he was spent. Were my sources of news out of touch with the political realities of the country?

Zuma had been deputy president of the country and was the front-runner for the top job, but seven months earlier, in June 2005, he had been unceremoniously sacked. The official reason was that his reputation had been tarnished. His friend, who was his financial advisor, had been found guilty of corruption and fraud, and it appeared Zuma was implicated too. The advisor got a 15-year sentence and the judge found 'overwhelming' evidence of a corrupt relationship between the two men.

The incumbent president, Thabo Mbeki, didn't have much time for Zuma anyway, and two weeks later he fired him. This created a political crisis which deepened when, a few months afterwards, Zuma was indicted on charges that included accepting bribes from a French arms company for defence contracts, and for corruption in connection with the advisor. He denied the charges.

And that wasn't all. Before the year was over, he was accused of rape. The allegation – which was never proved – captured the nation's attention for two reasons. First, it involved the 31-year-old daughter of one of his comrades. Her father, a freedom fighter, had been imprisoned with Zuma on Robben Island when Madiba was there too.

The other reason was that he knew she was HIV positive, and they'd had unprotected sex in his home. Zuma later explained that he took a shower afterwards to reduce the chance of infection. Given that South Africa had been ravaged by an epidemic of heterosexually transmitted HIV/AIDS, having a prominent person declare that a shower could be protective was beyond belief. It caused a national and international outcry.

HIV/AIDS was a burning issue, and Madiba too had been criticised for failing to understand the potential impact of this scourge. He had been president during a crucial time in the epidemic's evolution, and while nobody thought he could have stopped it, in retrospect some thought he could have taken a firm stand and used his moral power to reduce its impact. That he was busy with so many other things didn't absolve him.

For Zuma, 2005 ended badly. In December he was formally charged with rape and then his position as deputy president of the ANC was suspended pending his rape trial. He maintained his innocence, but the headlines declared that he was unlikely to recover, and the talk was that he would retreat from public view.

Now, barely a month later, his brief appearance at a petrol station was a sensation, and every person present would probably carry that story home with them that night. All this was swirling in my head as I walked into the cool of Madiba's house. I wanted to blurt it out, but seeing him sitting in his chair made me pause. This almost always happened. On seeing him again, I would feel a moment of grace.

As I stood in the doorway, his eyes lit up and he smiled. 'Good afternoon, doctor.' It meant so much to me that he always acknowledged me and seemed pleased I was there. After attending to his ears, I sensed a few empty moments, so I told him about my experience at the petrol station. Was there the slightest chance Zuma could become the next president after Mbeki? Madiba leaned back in his chair and looked at me. He was smiling. He paused for a long while and then wagged his finger at me, as he often did to drive a point home.

'No, doctor. Don't believe what you read in the newspapers or hear on the radio or watch on the television. Zuma will win in a landslide. And forget what you read in the Constitutional Court about him being sacked as deputy president. He will be the next president.'

Although Zuma had also been suspended as deputy president of the ANC, Madiba went on to predict that he would become president of that too. I looked at him aghast.

I can't remember the phrase he used, but he was saying Zuma had an 'X factor', an indefinable appeal, together with an ability to generate energy that people found irresistible. He had a high-voltage common touch. Madiba respected the people's admiration of Zuma and then he told me a story.

He and Zuma were slated to attend the same function. Madiba would walk in first, Zuma would follow, and they would make a joint appearance.

'Doctor, I am just an old man, and when I walked into that hall, people stood and clapped. When Zuma followed me, they got to their feet and ululated. They danced and screamed.'

As it happened, Zuma was prosecuted in the High Court and on 8 May 2006, the sex was deemed consensual and the rape charge was dismissed. He made a remarkable political comeback. Three years later, almost to the day, on 9 May 2009, he was elected president of South Africa.

One of the pleasures of going to Madiba's house was seeing Graça. As I arrived or left, sometimes we'd spend a few lovely minutes chatting at the door. She was warm and open, and we'd often talk about African politics and particularly health issues in South Africa and Mozambique. Graça had dedicated her life to international advocacy for women's and children's rights and had been Mozambique's first minister of education. Her report *The Impact of Armed Conflict on Children*, produced for United Nations Children's Fund (UNICEF), had influenced the United Nations' response in conflict zones. She would always leave me with something new and interesting. These encounters were relaxed and easy, and we'd exchange a few personal details too.

Until the last year or two of our relationship, my conversations with Madiba were never really personal. That wasn't his way. He operated on a different level and was concerned with principles and politics, not with the minor twists and turns of people's lives. Perhaps this was the effect of 27 years of relative isolation exclusively with men, of not being in a family or in a community where these matters are, of necessity, part of everyday discourse.

Once he was released from jail, he became a public personality and was never part of the social furniture of a room. When he was present, he was always the centre of attention, not because he wanted to be but because others made him so. There was little or no chit-chat, although he could be playful and a gentle tease. When he met my children, he engaged with them sweetly, even though they were overawed and tongue-tied.

We never talked about his family; I understood it was a protected domain. He had a grandson living with him, and as the boy was often playing in the study adjacent to the dining room, we became nodding acquaintances, but never more.

Then, in early 2005, Madiba's eldest son, Makgatho, died of AIDS. There were layers of tragedy in his passing. He was one of four children from Madiba's first marriage to Evelyn Mase and was the third to die. A daughter had passed away before her first birthday and another son was killed in a car crash while Madiba was on Robben Island. Despite a heart-felt plea, Madiba had been prohibited from attending the funeral.

On Makgatho's death, Madiba surprised the nation. He stepped up and frankly revealed the cause of death at a press conference. Prejudice against AIDS sufferers was so deep in the country that in those days people were ashamed to admit they had the disease. I watched that press conference. 'Let us give publicity to HIV/AIDS and not hide it, because the only way of making it appear to be a normal illness just like TB, like cancer, is always to come out and say somebody has died of HIV,' he said.

This was light years away from sentiments expressed by President Mbeki, who had challenged the link between HIV and AIDS and once reduced the issue to racism, claiming that whites regarded black people as 'rampant sexual beasts, unable to control our urges, unable to keep our legs crossed, unable to keep it in our pants'.

This kind of attitude had stymied efforts to manage the disease across the country, which, by then, had more than five million infected people, a number that was said to be higher than other African countries. In retrospect, this was probably spurious because South Africa just had better mechanisms for collecting statistics than the rest of the continent. There was also a lot of HIV denialism in other African countries.

Madiba and I talked a little about Makgatho and he told me he was proud of his son. There was no shame, and he felt his death could be a lesson to others. He was very keen for the youth of South Africa to be taught about HIV and to understand how to prevent and treat it.

By then he was an already powerful voice for an open and rational approach to HIV/AIDS. While people greatly appreciated this, they noted he had come to the cause too late to make a significant difference.

When he took office in 1994, HIV/AIDS was just taking hold in South Africa and was predicted to become enormous. At that point, they say, he could have shaped the country's response. He could have faced the threat squarely, employed available resources properly and used his moral authority to stamp out the stigma. While this wouldn't have prevented the pain, his clear thinking and his pragmatism could have lessened the suffering and the numbers of people affected. In retrospect, people said he was the only one who could have achieved this, but he missed the moment.

I saw it differently. In blunt terms, he spent the time between being released in 1990 and being elected president in 1994 not with his family, not having counselling to recover from the jail experience, but working around the clock to create a structure for the peaceful transition to majority rule. He was working to prevent a bloodbath.

When he became president, his agenda was chock-a-block. He was focused on running a country, ensuring military stability, maintaining reconciliation between racial groups, negotiating economic policies with disparate parties, keeping the mines functioning, electrifying settlements and revitalising international trade. He was bedding down the first democracy in the country and HIV/AIDS wasn't at the forefront of his consciousness.

After Madiba's term ended in mid-1999, Mbeki took the reins and created so much confusion in his management of HIV/AIDS that he became an international embarrassment. Southern Africa was the epicentre of the global epidemic, and his government was still refusing to supply antiretrovirals to prevent mother-to-child transmission.

In contrast, by 2000 Madiba had stepped up and begun campaigning and raising awareness. He called HIV/AIDS a silent, invisible enemy and exhorted people to be faithful to one partner and use a condom. In 2002, he wore an 'HIV Positive' T-shirt at a rally and became increasingly prominent in the fight against the epidemic and disinformation about it. These T-shirts were issued by the Treatment Action Campaign (TAC), a South African HIV/AIDS activist organisation co-founded by the HIV-positive activist Zackie Achmat in 1998.

In 2003, Madiba invited Linda and me to the first of a series of annual concerts he held to raise awareness of and funds for HIV/AIDS. These were called 46664 concerts (his prison number), and leading rock, pop and other superstar musicians of the day poured in. Everyone wanted to be involved and the stadiums were overflowing. We went to several concerts and were given wonderful seats near Madiba, and also went to 46664 fundraising lunches where we sat with international celebrities we never imagined we'd meet.

And we attended some of the annual lectures held in his name, usually delivered by a distinguished speaker. We were unapologetic devotees, keen and hugely encouraged by his stand, which was contrary to the government's position. He was promoting humanity and the reality and science of the disease. He was popularising it and trying to strip it of its stigma.

Madiba's disposition was serious, and whenever we talked about HIV/AIDS, his tone became more solemn. He told me emphatically that he was not in favour of the views of the health minister and the president. While many European, Arab, Asian and African leaders shied away from the topic, he was never afraid to speak his mind.

In 2006, the year Makgatho died, there was an international AIDS conference in Toronto. To general disbelief, South Africa's exhibition stand was dominated by unproven nutritional remedies such as beetroot, with almost no reference to evidence-based medication. Shortly afterwards, 80 prominent international scientists wrote an open letter to Mbeki calling on him to sack his health minister whom they blamed for 'disastrous, pseudo-scientific policies' on HIV/AIDS.

After Mbeki resigned as president in 2008, a new health minister committed the government to a scientific and decisive response to the epidemic.

CHAPTER 20

My brother, my leader

E ARLY IN 2008, a radio report about Libya caught my attention. I turned the volume up. The newsreader was saying that Libya had taken the presidency of the UN Security Council for a month. This was startling: Libya's swaggering leader, Colonel Muammar Gaddafi, was known for having people 'disappear' and for sending his hit squads to wipe out his opponents in exile. Then there was that dark massacre of 1 200 prisoners in a maximum-security prison in Tripoli. Libya had long been a pariah state. Obviously, I'd missed the turnaround.

Madiba was close to Gaddafi and had remained loyal to him through many turbulent years. In South Africa, this friendship had been frowned upon, and some notable world leaders had condemned it outright, but Madiba held fast. I was due to see him later that morning and hoped to get an opportunity to ask him about this.

When Shamim and I went to see him together, we went in and out relatively quickly. Once our jobs were done, we didn't hang around. But when I went alone, I never knew if I would be there for 15 minutes – about the time it took to manage his ears – or whether he'd offer me tea because he had time to chat. This day, fortune smiled on me. He was sitting in the lounge and, as usual, greeted me warmly. 'Ah, doctor, it's so good of you to come and see me.' I attended to his ears and, as I packed up my kit, we chatted about this and that. When there was no one around, I asked him about this latest piece of news.

'Would you like some tea?' he asked.

'Well, if you have the time.'

'No, not at all,' he replied – his way of saying, 'It's a pleasure.'

Whenever I stayed on, I was conscious of not over-staying. At any moment, one of his intimidating minders could come in, shoot me a stern look and announce another appointment. I didn't want to take advantage of Madiba, nor to be thought to be doing so.

As he spoke, I settled into a comfortable chair and soon Mary, his personal secretary, came in with a tray. She put down the familiar silver pot, two bone china cups and a few biscuits. While I loved this ritual, after almost seven years I still felt slightly awkward about having this extraordinary opportunity adjacent to my professional responsibilities. Madiba would be turning 90 that July and these were precious moments.

We started with the Lockerbie disaster almost 20 years earlier. In December 1988, a bomb exploded on a Pan Am flight over the Scottish town of Lockerbie – parts of the plane crashed into a residential street and 270 people lost their lives. This was the deadliest terror attack in British history and, before 9/11, the biggest for the US.

Although Madiba was still behind bars at the time, he had access to newspapers and would have read about this disaster. He wasn't so much interested in talking about the actual event as in the international negotiations that followed. He played a key role in that period and as he began to describe what had happened, I got the briefest glimpse of what had made him such an extraordinary negotiator.

Libya was a prime suspect in the bombing. Three years after the crash, following a lengthy investigation, arrest warrants were issued for two Libyan nationals. But Gaddafi would not admit culpability and would not hand over the men. When sanctions were successively piled on his country, he didn't budge, and a decade after the crash he still hadn't given up the men. Madiba was working away in the background, talking to him and others, trying to break the deadlock. He wasn't alone in this.

For most people, Madiba was a benign elder with a conciliatory tone. They never got to feel the steel just below his skin. Yes, he was the father of the nation – an old man full of grace – but he was also highly strategic and would not bend to anyone's will unless he believed, with complete conviction, that they were right.

He saw the world through different eyes and, because of his moral authority, very few were able to challenge him while he was in power. In his frail final years, and once he'd passed away, people were bolder with their criticism.

That morning, however, he was animated. The discussion wasn't warm; it was principled and left me full of admiration and relief that I had never and would never come up against him. It was different to our previous chats. This was no gently unfolding parable. He was purposeful, instructing me.

While his overriding principle was that things must be fair, he understood that human nature is never simple. He had disciplined himself not to judge people and said negotiations were between human beings, not angels. He often repeated that he was not an angel, and he didn't know anyone who was. Anyway, angelic status was slippery. I can see him leaning forward and saying how a man elevated as an angel in the West could be regarded as a devil in the East. With the reverse being true too, he didn't care for such characterisations.

Much to the chagrin of the West, Madiba had trumpeted his support for the Libyan leader. And the refrain was the same: Gaddafi had supported South Africa's liberation struggle while the great democracies had supported the apartheid regime. Months after his release from prison in 1990, Madiba flew to Libya to thank Gaddafi. Then, in 1994, he invited Gaddafi to South Africa to attend his inauguration as president. He gave short shrift to anyone who looked askance.

Their relationship was strong and in 1997, while quietly working on the Lockerbie negotiation, he visited Libya again, hugged Gadaffi and kissed him on each cheek, saying, 'My brother leader, my leader, how nice to see you.' The Western press went berserk. The great Mandela was hugging the great murderer – that prison massacre was still fresh in the international mind. Madiba stood firm and told the press he was unimpressed by America's opposition to this mission. 'Those who say I should not be here are without morals. I am not going to join them in their lack of morality,' he said.

*

While Madiba's acknowledgement of Gaddafi was causing uncomfortable waves in public, in private he was developing a plan that would dump the British government's decision to put the two men on trial in Scotland, where the 270 deaths had occurred. The British argued that as the tragedy happened there, and it was the place where feeling ran high, it was appropriate the trial should be held there.

Madiba saw it differently. If the two Libyan suspects were to be released to stand trial, he said it should be conducted in a neutral venue. He knew this would not be popular, but from his own experience, he also knew what it would mean for them to be tried in Scotland, in a Western system, with a Western judge, a Western jury and Western legal teams. The implications would be complex.

Behind the scenes, the British argued that holding it in a neutral country would require primary legislation and, given all the procedural complications, the risk of collapse was high. Couldn't the matter of fairness simply be covered by inviting international observers to attend a trial in Scotland? Madiba shook his head.

He told me he knew the British Foreign Office and Prime Minister Tony Blair were annoyed at his involvement in the negotiations and felt he should butt out. In the plainest language, with no hype, he was telling me about manoeuvres on the international stage, just as he might tell me about a backyard dispute between neighbours. He made it sound so simple.

There was one piece of information he didn't tell me, that I have since learned. Recently released archives show that when the Foreign Office discovered Madiba was visiting Libya en route to the Commonwealth Heads of Government (CHOGM) Meeting in Edinburgh in October 1997, it was alarmed and warned of trouble if he spoke out against plans to hold the trial in Scotland.

Classified documents reveal that Blair attempted to prevent him from raising the issue. In a handwritten memo to Madiba, he urged him not to raise his preference for a neutral venue:

'Lockerbie is of course a particularly sensitive subject in Scotland because of the deaths on the ground of 11 inhabitants of the small town of Lockerbie, in addition to the 259 people on board the aircraft. So, I hope we can avoid a discussion of the issue at CHOGM itself – we have a lot of other things to talk about. But I would welcome further private discussions when we meet next week.'

Although suspicious of each other in Edinburgh, Madiba and Blair hugged in public. The press went berserk again. But when Madiba stood up to speak, he pointedly ignored Blair's request and disclosed his plan. He asserted that that no one nation should be a complainant, prosecutor and judge. He had all but won the day.

The following month, the UK House of Commons was told that as Mandela held unquestioned prestige for what he had achieved, it behoved the House to listen to what he said on what might be an awkward subject. The House was urged to consider seriously the idea of holding the trial in a third, neutral country.

The following year, Madiba took a swipe at US President

Clinton, whose disapproval of Gaddafi was well known. Standing next to Clinton at a news conference, Madiba expressed that he would not have his loyalty to the Libyan challenged:

'I have also invited Brother Leader Gaddafi to this country. And I do that because our moral authority dictates that we should not abandon those who helped us in the darkest hour in the history of this country ... Not only did the Libyans support us in return, they gave us the resources for us to conduct our struggle, and to win. And those South Africans who have berated me for being loyal to our friends can literally go and jump into a pool.'

According to the *Los Angeles Times*, Clinton didn't flinch. He stood smiling beside Madiba. And he had good reason to smile – negotiations on a compromise were underway. A hybrid solution was later agreed: the trial would be held in the Netherlands, governed by Scottish law. With this in place, Madiba went back to Gaddafi to negotiate the handover of the two men in April 1999.

One was convicted. Former Libyan intelligence officer Abdelbaset al-Megrahi was found guilty in 2001 of mass murder, sentenced to life in prison and later released on medical grounds. In 2023, an older man, Abu Agila Masud, was captured and extradited to the US after confessing in 2013, while in Libyan custody, to having built and delivered the bomb.

Our conversation about Libya had lasted about 45 minutes. No one had disturbed us and although I was intrigued and reluctant to leave, it was time to go. I always tried to leave before being asked. So I stood, took his hand and wished him well, saying – as I usually did – that he should call any time he needed me, and anyway, I'd see him at our next appointment. As I turned to go, I noticed my tea had gone cold.

Walking back to my car, I felt I'd understood something new and replayed bits of the conversation in my mind. The exchange was exciting because his thinking was so unusual. He would travel through several layers to find the human being in a negotiation.

First came the big picture. Here he recognised that Libya had committed atrocities, but he never believed that the Western powers and colonialists had a blameless past. This didn't neutralise the context of the negotiation, but it made operating within it much easier. Nobody had a pure history, and no country could claim to be the policeman of the world.

Next, he seemed to be able separate people from politics. Here were two suspects, schooled in a dictatorship and believing in its ideology. They were about to be tried by people born into a liberal democracy who were convinced that their legal institutions were morally superior.

Third, he took the biblical step of separating the individual from their behaviour. This is in line with the ancient wisdom that says that while God loves all his children, it doesn't mean he loves what they do. Rather than seeing people as inherently evil, Madiba saw them as behaving differently, or badly. While no one was an angel, almost no one was beyond reform.

He was also concerned about the influence that the angry and bereaved families of Lockerbie could carry in a local courtroom.

This three-step process of reaching the person does

not come naturally to most of us, and certainly not to me. Unlike Madiba, most of us are not capable of seeing the individual in the sweep of international affairs.

Back on Robben Island, through the bars of his cell, he had seen the person inside the guard uniform. He recognised the humanity of one of his jailers, James Gregory; in turn, Gregory recognised that he'd been seen, and responded. Together they built a friendship. Madiba had transcended the jailer-prisoner divide from the inside of his cell, and as a free man he was able to rise above the confines of conventional international diplomacy.

CHAPTER 21

Staring into the sun

A S THE SEASONS rolled by, my relationship with Madiba grew a little more personal. It sounds contradictory, but while he was always warm and present, internally he remained fortified. I neither expected nor tried to grow close, but familiarity did ease things and I could sense he trusted me more. He would confide in me about his other health concerns, talk a little more about his family and ask about mine. While these conversations were a touch more intimate, he never changed the way he addressed me. It was always 'doctor' or, on the very rare occasions that my children were present, 'your father'.

I was keen for Linda and our children to have a few moments with him, for history, for memory and for the experience of his presence. They had all met him in my consulting rooms and although he was unfailingly friendly, the children were barely able to speak if he addressed them.

In one of these brief encounters, he wrote notes to each of my twin daughters, encouraging them for their future education. Each now keeps their note safe.

After that meeting, one of the twins, Yael, wrote an account of it for a school project. She was 12 at the time and described the anticipation of sitting in her father's rooms with her sister Leora and Linda, waiting for him to arrive:

'Would you like to open the door for Mandela when he arrives?' my dad's secretary, Sandy, asked me.

'No, thanks. I'm too nervous.' ... I heard his footsteps approaching with many others of his bodyguards. I could hear his sweet sincere voice growing louder and louder. As he walked through the door, I froze. There he was, a man I'd only seen on television and a man whom I respected and adored ...

... from the second he stepped in the room, a warm and tranquil energy just like his personality filled the air. It was like seeing an angel except Mandela was a human being. His face was glowing brightly.

It was as if I was staring into the sun. He stood tall and I could feel a sense of pride. He was wearing one of his traditional informal shirts. It was gold and a design of leaves was imprinted on it. He was also wearing an AIDS awareness badge.

As he greeted me, I noticed his eyes were a greyish blue like the colour of the sea on a cold and windy day ...

That was in late 2003, when he was 85. He'd held up well but over the next few years, his strength noticeably began to ebb. Although weaker and with his engagement with the wider world diminishing, he didn't want his health to slide and understandably wanted his hearing to be as clear as it could be. Age-related hearing loss is usually progressive and his was deteriorating. I also noticed that, as with most octogenarians, his short-term memory was not as sharp as it had been when I'd first met him. I could feel him growing old and our encounters seemed more precious.

One morning I got a late request to be at the house at lunchtime, with Shamim, to attend to his ears ahead of an important meeting early that afternoon. Despite this meeting, I knew it was a quiet time of year for him, and spontaneously – and rather boldly – I asked his minder if my two younger children could come along with us.

Permission was granted, so I called my sons' primary school, picked up Aharon and Benjamin at the gate and promised to return them after the lunch break. The boys were flabbergasted as we were shown through security and walked past the idle motorcade and up to the house. We were ushered into the dining room where Madiba was having lunch alone. An empty plate of lamb curry was being cleared away. As I stood beside him to clean one ear, Shamim sat on the other side to check and reset his hearing aid. Then we swapped. For a moment, like statues, the boys stood in their school uniforms, their eyes fixed on Madiba. He smiled at them, motioned for them to come closer and shook their hands. As Aharon, then age 11, now 27, still remembers this in detail, I'll leave it to him to describe:

> I remember walking through the door and the first thing I saw was a massive portrait of him and Graça.

Then we turned into the dining room and there he was, in the flesh. I was starstruck, in complete disbelief that the actual real Mandela was just sitting there. To me he had been a superhero, a giant figure, not a real person.

I first saw him from behind. He was at the table, sitting in a big armchair. He was so tall; his iconic grey hair was popping over the top of the chair and I could see part of his golden paisley shirt.

When my dad introduced us I was too anxious to speak, but when Mandela offered me his massive hand, I did manage to shake it. I noticed his feet were swollen and couldn't quite fit into his slip-on shoes. He was preparing his dessert, and I watched his huge hands cut up a mango.

Through a glass door to the side, I could see into the next room where one of his grandsons was wearing sneakers and playing on a PlayStation, in view of his grandfather. It was surreal. In this setting Mandela seemed to be just an ordinary grandfather.

He asked us our names and when I told him mine was Aharon, he noted it was a biblical name. He invited me to sit down on one side, right next to him with Benji sitting next to me. Did we intend to become doctors too? he inquired.

Then smiling, he announced that 'when you qualify as a doctor, I'm going to dismiss your father and you're going to be my new doctor.' As we were about to leave, he remarked that Benjamin was from the Bible too.

'When I go to heaven, they will ask me, What is your name?, and I will say I'm Madiba. And they will say from where? And I'll say from South Africa, and they'll say where's that? Who are you? We don't know you.

'But you and Benjamin are from the Bible, so you will be invited in. So please, will you put in a good word for me in heaven?'

We left feeling great.

For our children, a Madiba moment like this was unrepeatable and lifted them above the daily insecurities of their existence. The reality, however, was that they lived in fear.

CHAPTER 22

He listened but did not comment

BY 2008, OUR HOUSE was a suburban fortress. But even with security gates, high walls topped with spikes and electric wires, cameras, alarms, panic buttons and CAP on call at a moment's notice, none of us felt safe. The passage to the bedrooms was gated, but during the night some of the children still dragged their bedding to our room. If the alarm happened to be set off accidentally, they took it as a signal of an invasion and shot out of their beds. In minutes armed security guards arrived with dogs. In the noise and chaos, it's no wonder they could never be sure what was happening. Unfortunately, my obsession with safety had been transferred to them. Had I been more insulated, say, in an office job, our household could have been calmer.

When Linda and I went out together, the children worried about us. One weekend, the two of us were on our way to visit my mother when I sensed we were being tailed. The rear-view mirror told me all I needed to know. It also told the hijackers I knew. They peeled off and a red car slipped into their place. I was about to turn into my mother's town-house complex where there would be a pause at the security gate. I didn't turn. Later that day, CAP reported a couple of hijackings with a red car of the same description.

There were too many near misses for my liking and I felt the odds were shortening. My weekly debriefing sessions with a psychologist were barely enough for me to cope. I was on perpetual standby, with no promise of the pressure lightening.. It wasn't just needing to deal with injuries or comforting patients, many of whom didn't survive, or if they did, were left with terrible disabilities; it was something thing else. It was walking the short distance from the theatre to a room where the uncertain but still hopeful family had been waiting for hours. Hope keeps the head up, and if the news was crushing, I'd pause outside, take a deep breath, and then go in. This never got easier. When you see other people's eyes well up, it's hard to keep your own dry. Then you leave them with nothing but grief.

I was just holding myself together when something happened that broke me in pieces.

On Monday evenings, to try and bring some normalcy to our marriage and to dedicate some time to ourselves, Linda and I used to go to a Latin American dance class. On Monday, 28 January 2008, I was getting into the car when my brother-in-law, Mark, called to say there had been a shooting at the football grounds, a kilometre away. An old school friend of mine had been shot in the car park. As coach, Mark had kept the children on the field.

It was high summer, about 7 o'clock, and an other-wise ordinary evening in Highlands North, a suburb of Johannesburg minutes from where I and most of the other parents lived. I'd grown up on these football grounds and knew the park well; it had always been a happy place for me. But as I drove in, the horror was right there in front of me. My friend was slumped forward in the driver's seat of his SUV. Despite all my efforts, he remained unresponsive.

I have no words for what followed and can only relay the events mechanically. First his children came running off the field. Then his father drove in, took in what had happened and drove into a wall. Then his wife arrived with their little girl. They were inconsolable.

I stayed back until the police came and did their work and the mortuary van arrived. All the while, he was in my arms, and I found myself saying prayers. Although dark, it was a clear night, the full moon was waning and I was look-ing to the heavens. I knew it was over for me. I had to get my children out. There was no more debate. Something had died in me. There and then, from the depths of my being, I made an oath that I would be out of the country in a year.

When I got home at 11:30 pm, Linda was waiting for me. Although beyond distraught, I managed to tell her that something had broken in me and described my vow. She listened and then, with care, reminded me that we had been through this before. She reassured me that I would be able to work through it all in therapy. It would fade with time. I would be okay. Without regard to the time difference, I picked up the phone and called my sister in Sydney, told her what had happened and said I would be overseas within a year. Then I all but went silent. I could barely function. For the next six weeks I hardly spoke, other than in therapy.

Over time things sort of normalised, but in my bones I knew I'd taken the final blow. As close as was humanly possible, I'd seen the impact on my friend's children, and I couldn't bring myself even to imagine my children having to confront such darkness. I would do everything I could to protect them from the possibility. It transpired that the gunmen were hijacking someone else in the car park, saw my school friend on his phone, assumed he was calling for help, and shot him. But it wasn't so. While waiting for his sons to complete training, he'd been chatting to his father on his phone. When the line went dead and the connection couldn't be restored, his father got into his own car. My friend was shot through the neck and the post-mortem showed he died immediately. That this had happened just the other side of the CAP boundary shook me.

All I could think of was my parental responsibility to my five children. I had to keep them safe and give them the opportunity to grow unharmed into adulthood. Once they had received citizenship elsewhere, I would have fulfilled my duty, and if as adults they decided to return to South Africa, then so be it.

By mid-March, I was back in the world and telling everyone I was planning to leave. Nobody believed me. We'd all been through moments when we threw up our hands and said we were going, but so many of us stayed. Neither my wife nor my twin brother nor my parents-in-law believed we'd go. Apart from my mother, who thought it was best for us to leave, no one else took me seriously. For a while, I didn't take myself sufficiently seriously either, forgetting

I was in my mid-forties and imagining it would be easy to get a job somewhere else.

I told Madiba what had happened, how shaken I was and how I felt driven to get my children to safety. I didn't need to talk about the previous two episodes and the cumulative effect. His family had been subjected to unrelenting violence and he knew what I was saying. On one or two previous occasions, I had mentioned to him that I was considering leaving. He heard but let it pass. This time, however, he listened very carefully and gave me the gift of his presence.

CHAPTER 23

Setting an example

FOR THE FIRST MONTHS after that shooting, my resolve to take my children to a safer country was rock hard. I tolerated no debate. But as time passed, it began to soften. I didn't really want to leave and was in continual conflict with myself. As I parked outside my well-equipped consulting rooms, I thought, Why give all this up? My practice was busy, I was head of the ENT department and, at last, I was doing relevant research. Professionally, I couldn't have been happier. But driving home, I'd hear something on the radio and think 'Oh my God, I've got to get the family out as fast as possible.'

Then I'd turn into our tree-lined street, greet our guard, park indoors, and sit down to dinner with Linda and our children on the terrace. The garden was in bloom, the pool sparkled and the dogs lay at our feet. But once it got dark, terror crept into our hearts.

At dawn, we bounced back. We were all born in South Africa, the country was in our blood and we had the best of it. It sounds excessive – and it was – but by then we owned a time-share in a game lodge a couple of hours away, and we'd pile into our SUV, drive north and spend the weekend in the bush. We had binoculars, we had reference books about African game, and at the lodge we shared an open, olive-green game-viewing vehicle with tiered seats. Bumping over tracks to waterholes was thrilling for the children. For all of us, there was no better holiday. We'd be out before sunrise, breathing in the addictive dawn scent of the African bush and watching the animals wake.

In the summer we'd drive south to our other time-share at San Lameer golf estate on the coast, near Margate, where security was excellent. The large, comfortable house had a pool to cool off, there was space for friends to stay and a long stretch of safe beach, and, most importantly, the children could all roam free.

When our children were still small, Mike Plitt gave Linda a piece of advice. He and his wife, who was also a doctor, worked punishing hours and made a point of taking two good holidays a year with their children. 'All they will remember are these holidays,' he told Linda definitively. As we worked long hours too, she was enthusiastic about the idea and would arrange lots of time away. She wanted the seven of us to build joyous memories together. Linda is highly energetic and as her timetable was more flexible than mine, she would often drive down with the kids alone, a week ahead of me. I'd arrive to a relaxed family that was genuinely pleased to see me.

But what use were memories if you could, at any point, suddenly be shot?

As soon as I got a grip on myself, I started job-hunting everywhere. I applied for registration wherever I could and was ready to take anything, at any level. I'd looked many times before, but this time there were even fewer openings. I fretted daily. Should we go, shouldn't we go? This dilemma played out in my relationships at home and at work, and I became more impossible than usual. My colleagues kept rolling their eyes. 'You'll get over it,' they said. 'Eventually we all get over it and you will too, as you've done in the past.'

There were so many reasons to stay. Linda and I were doing worthwhile philanthropic work, our eldest son was excelling at university, and for the other children, their school was another home. We had a large extended family, long-standing friends and we lived in a tight-knit community. In the face of external threats, communities look inward, grow closer and the quality of life within them changes. We understood without words and we knew that together we could withstand more. So, when an international removals truck parked outside one of the houses and started loading up, a tremor went through our community.

Personally, a major reason to stay was that the two most important elders in my life, my mother and Madiba, were in their last years. I never wanted to leave them. So shouldn't we just stay on for a little a while? Perhaps a few years? No, because then I would be 50. Although I could never recreate all that we had, with the energy of these few years I still had a chance of creating a modest alternative. Also, by going soon, the risk to the family would be lessened.

During this period of personal anguish, Madiba, as

always, showed me another way of being. I never witnessed him allowing his personal conflicts to weigh on others. Every time I saw him, I had an opportunity to learn about self-mastery. I recognised this in him, and I could see its value, but I was not a good student. It would take me many more years to practise it myself.

In July that year he would be turning 90. He was tired, he had underlying health issues, and all he really wanted was a quiet, private celebration with his family in the small rural village of Qunu. But people around the world wanted to celebrate this significant birthday too. So he found the energy.

For those abroad, he arranged one type of celebration. For his local friends, who were also determined to celebrate, he arranged another, and for his closest and dearest, he reserved the actual day, 18 July 2008, for a gathering at Qunu. The effort required for these three events would be enormous, but everyone's desires would be accommodated.

For the world, he turned one of his famous 46664 concerts – designed to raise awareness of and funds for HIV/AIDS – into a birthday celebration. Some 46 664 tickets to London's Hyde Park were up for sale. The event was televised and millions more watched as a parade of superstars displayed their talents. To thunderous applause, Madiba went on stage to thank everyone.

Although he rose to the occasion and put on a brave front, I knew he was pushing himself. He told me that this no longer felt like a meaningful celebration of his birthday, but there were other reasons he wanted to make the trip. While he was still in jail in 1988, his seventieth birthday had been marked in his absence with a concert at Wembley Stadium.

Now he wanted to use this opportunity to acknowledge, by his presence at a concert in London, all those who had participated in the Free Nelson Mandela campaign back then, and particularly those souls who had stood vigil outside the South African embassy for him. He never forgot them, and despite his old bones, I saw him summon his life force and recreate that spirit of the past.

Most of all, he was looking forward to the intimate gathering at Qunu, his touchstone and the place where he finally wanted to rest in peace. The day after this family gathering, he would host 500 guests at a party with an extraordinary mix of local villagers, elders, members of African royalty, presidents, old comrades, lawyers and friends. Linda and I were invited. I had long wanted to go to Qunu, and as we prepared for the trip, I managed to put my migration mania in abeyance. I didn't want anything to interfere with my appreciation of Madiba at this milestone, at the place on earth where he felt most comfortable.

CHAPTER 24

Pilgrimage

L INDA AND I SPENT the night in Port Edward, and
in the early hours of the morning we wrapped up
warmly and set out, navigating our way into the
Transkei by moonlight. Progress was slow, not only because
of potholes but because cows, goats and the occasional horse
strayed onto the road. As the sun began to rise in the eastern
African sky, we fell into silence. It felt like a pilgrimage.

We wound through small villages waking for the day,
with early plumes of smoke and small signs of human activity around the dwellings. Outside it was close to freezing,
the roads were untarred and the air dusty. As the winter sun
rose it gradually got warmer, and three hours or so later we
found ourselves within view of the 'big town' of Umtata
(today Mthatha), our first stop. Here we had to find a place
to change into our traditional African attire and we bumped
into others on the same mission.

We had not been to this part of the country before and took in the naked hills of the Transkei and the traditional kraals. We saw women carrying loads on their heads and round Xhosa huts dotted through the landscape. From the car, the land looked calm and quiet. Our reverie was broken when, on a hill in front of us, we suddenly saw a single-storey brick home. With its low wall and modern fittings, it looked completely out of place. As we approached, police were everywhere. They instructed us to park on the nearby dirt road and walk up to the house.

No one was allowed into the house. Guests were met personally by Mandla Mandela, Madiba's grandson and chief of the area. We were given orange-and-turquoise beaded necklaces with a wooden pendant bearing the emblem of the Mandela clan. Then ululating young women invited us into a tea garden in front of a huge marquee. Some guests were in beaded traditional skins, some had feathers, and some wore T-shirts emblazoned with Mandela's face. A few, like us, were in more muted local dress.

I knew several of Madiba's friends and was chatting to one of his original lawyers when Zelda walked by. It had been some time since I'd seen Madiba, and I had brought my medical equipment with me, just in case. Zelda agreed it would be a good idea to check his ears and hearing aids before the function began.

With permission granted, I walked around to the entrance of the house where people would usually arrive. What struck me immediately was that the entrance looked very similar to a photograph I'd seen of the warder's cottage in the grounds of Victor Verster prison (now Klein Drakenstein), where Madiba had been held for six years after leaving Robben Island. The house was modern and, in the setting, stood out as the residence of a wealthy and important person. It did not have natural appeal but the obvious similarity to his old jail was puzzling.

Inside he was sitting quietly, his cane next to him. He recognised me and gave that smile. 'Good morning and happy birthday,' I said, shaking his hand. 'I'm here to check your ears before the party.' Gracious as ever, he gave me the response I knew so well. 'No, doctor, that is very good. I appreciate it because it is important that I hear what people are saying.' When I'd finished, he thanked me again, and with a predictability that warmed my heart, he said, 'Now I am going to hear everything I'm not supposed to hear.'

'May I ask you something?'

He nodded.

'When I look at this house, it looks very similar to the warder's cottage at Victor Verster. Is it so?'

'No, doctor, you are correct. I did not want this house to be built for me. I wanted to live in my old village. And I didn't want the ANC and the government to put this fancy house up on the hill when there's so much poverty here.'

It had been 14 years since the ANC had taken power, and for most people in that region there was still no running water, no electricity and no tarred roads. Madiba wasn't finished: 'They did this against my wishes. They said I needed this. So, I ensured that the entrance of this house would always remind me of where I came from. Whenever I entered this house, as grateful as I would feel, I would never forget my origins.'

Outside, the herdboys started beating drums to signal the beginning of the festivities. It was time to go.

Although Madiba looked good at his party and had given a small group of journalists an interview the day before, to me he seemed spiritually fatigued. He'd outlived his peers and, watching him that day, I realised that when you are the last of your generation, you are in a solitary place. There was not a living soul present who had known him as a boy or seen him grow up. Of course, family and friends were around and Graça was lovingly by his side, but he was at the end of a long road.

In some of our conversations he had told me he was tired and ready to pass on. Two of his closest and dearest friends, Walter Sisulu and Oliver Tambo, had died. These were men he knew at almost a cellular level. They had such commonality of background and such mutual understanding that no words had to pass between them.

It is noteworthy that these three Xhosa men passed away at ten-year intervals: Tambo in 1993, Sisulu in 2003 and Madiba in 2013. In those 20 years, much of the energy of South Africa's resistance generation passed too. The three had given their adult lives to the struggle. Madiba would have spent more time with Sisulu and Tambo than with his family, and while their companionship wasn't a substitute, there was something powerful in it. There were times when they almost depended on each other for survival. They were comrades-in-arms. Sisulu was his confidant in prison and Tambo was his lifeline to the world.

Madiba and Tambo were born a year apart, in the same geography, and Tambo too began life herding cattle. Both went to the University of Fort Hare, and with Sisulu's encouragement the two co-founded the African National Congress Youth League. They couldn't have been closer when they opened South Africa's first black law firm together. The way the cards fell, while Madiba went to prison, Tambo went into a 30-year exile. He returned late in the year that Madiba was released, but by then he was ill. He suffered strokes in 1989 and 1991 and was robbed of his speech. They had just over two years together before he died of a heart attack at the age of 75. He never lived to see Madiba become president.

I remembered how Sisulu's death left Madiba with an unfillable hole. He regarded him as a brother. They were bonded in shared experience: both had been herdboys in the Transkei and the older Sisulu was the first to introduce Madiba to the ANC. Through their resolute commitment to the struggle, they were imprisoned on Robben Island together and later moved to Pollsmoor Prison together. After liberation, Sisulu declined a position in government but shared his wisdom as an advisor to Madiba.

These three men had made a conscious choice to work for the greater good. I don't know about the personal lives of the other two, but for Madiba, his family paid a high price. He wasn't averse to talking about these moral complexities and once said to me – as he had to others – that yes, people loved him, but from afar. Those close to him saw him differently. The public might hero-worship him, but his family knew the real man. They knew how he had suffered and how they, too, had suffered.

It occurred to me that I was seeing the wear and tear of heroism. It was the closest I'd ever been to a public hero, and I could see that, for him, being worshipped was draining rather than sustaining. There was little authentic, shared communication because adulation is a one-way street. Yes, there was plenty of acknowledgement of what he had been through, but the ongoing complexities of his personal condition were not addressed – and he kept it that way. As Madiba grew frailer, there was still lots of adoration from the public and those around him but much less meaningful conversation.

My memory of those last years is misted in sadness. I think of the multi-layered decisions he'd had to make in his life, and that he'd had so much time locked away from loved ones and then no time to repair his neglected relationships. While being swept up by the greater good was glorious and politically fulfilling, it was also emotionally impoverishing.

But his inner life was not a concern for the public and, like so many others, I often thought of how much more of an impact he might have had, how much more might have been achieved, and how much more might have lasted the distance had he been released earlier.

CHAPTER 25

The third phone call

ONE EVENING IN 2008, at about 8 o'clock I received a call on my mobile from Graça. She couldn't get hold of Mike Plitt, so she phoned me. 'Dr Friedland, I'm sorry to disturb you but would you mind coming to check on Madiba. I'm concerned about him, and I don't want my concern to get into the newspapers.' I said, 'With pleasure,' and told Linda I would be back soon.

'I'm definitely coming with you; you can't leave me at home,' she said. Although Linda had come to the Mandela residence with me before, this time I protested: 'But Linda, you haven't been invited! You know how careful I am not to push the boundaries and not to abuse my position. He's busy, he's getting older, he's tired. I won't spend much time there.'

Whenever Linda had accompanied me in the past, I'd always encouraged her to keep it short. Madiba, for his part, was very generous with his time, and gracious whenever Linda was in the room. 'Doctor,' he would say, 'I don't know what you've done to deserve such a beautiful woman, and such a young woman.' And then he would say, 'Linda, would you like a cup of tea?' I'd say no, no, thank you, we really have to go, but Linda would say she'd love a cup. Then, of course, the fine china cups and silver pots would promptly arrive.

My relationship with Madiba was warm but straightforward. He knew I would never ask for a favour, I would not flatter him, I would not bring gifts and I wouldn't ask him to appear at any of my social functions. And this evening, particularly given the circumstances – I had no idea what was wrong – I felt I should go alone. However, I just couldn't keep Linda away.

When we arrived, we went straight through the security gate and got to the front door, which was closed. I knocked and Graça opened it. She'd been waiting for me. Sheepishly, I explained that my wife had wanted to come too and would happily wait downstairs. 'Sure, I'll give her a cup of tea,' Graça said. I looked pleadingly at Linda, imploring her to decline. But Linda, who is abundantly social, was already engaged in deep conversation with Graça. As they went off together, Graça pointed in the direction of the stairs, giving me brief directions and saying Madiba was expecting me.

This was the first time I had been upstairs. I followed the directions to the bedroom and felt as if I was about to enter the Holy of Holies, where a great soul slept. I walked in and saw a queen-sized bed with the covers rolled back. There was no one in the room. To the left, on the bedside table, were Madiba's neatly folded spectacles, his fountain pen and his hearing aids, all in a straight row, military style. There was also a copy of the latest *Time* magazine, with a beautiful photograph of him on the cover. It was the 21 July 2008 edition and he was wearing the hearing aids with the brown moulds that Shamim had made for him. Our handiwork was on the cover of *Time* magazine! (In 2012, those hearing aids would make another unexpected appearance on a series of South African bank notes, probably the first time hearing aids had appeared on the country's official currency.)

Aware that no one had sourced the magazine for him, I had brought Madiba that copy of *Time* and felt pleased he had it so close. The cover line celebrated him at 90 and offered readers the opportunity to discover the secrets of his leadership. I had a copy too and had already been through it. I remembered the first secret: 'Courage is not the absence of fear – it's inspiring others to move beyond it.'

As I didn't know where Madiba was, I sat on a chair at the end of the bed and waited. Then I heard the toilet flush. And I thought to myself, 'Oh my God, this man is a human being.' After sitting beside him for so many years, seeing him eat, laugh, dance and get angry, it was indeed an odd realisation. A couple of minutes later, he shuffled through in his dressing gown. He looked at me and said, 'Good evening, doctor. Thank you for coming to see this old man at such a late hour. I appreciate it very much.' I was taken by the fact that even at night, he maintained his dignity. He was immaculate, his pyjamas fresh and uncreased beneath his dressing gown.

He sat on his bed and explained the problem he had. By that time, I was well accustomed to examining him.

I knew the shape of his head and ears intimately; I'd shaken his hand uncountable times and often held his arm as we walked. But this examination was different to our regular consultations, where Madiba was dressed and going about his day, ready to engage. I examined him in his pyjamas, and as a doctor I was aware of how clothes and physical position influence perception. When a person is well dressed, sitting comfortably and conversing with confidence, you are less likely to notice the vulnerabilities that lie behind this presentation. Of course, I knew Madiba was growing weaker spiritually. Increasingly, our conversations had touched on loss. Occasionally, I felt a wistfulness in him. As the last survivor of a generation, he was missing the comrades who had kept him going through difficult years. But now, as I examined him, I was struck by how tired he was physically too. At 90, the great engine was slowing.

I finished my examination and reassured him that I didn't believe it was anything serious and that it could wait until the morning. Then I called Graça, who left Linda and came upstairs. I explained my findings to her. She was very grateful. Madiba got into bed and put on his glasses. I looked at him. He was resting.

That image is lodged in my mind, for ever.

CHAPTER 26

A toenail in the door

MY GRAND PROMISE to myself – to be out of South Africa before 28 January 2009 – was looking shaky. Despite much effort, by September 2008 I hadn't secured a job and was worried. We were in the teeth of the global financial crisis and there seemed to be caution all around. In July, a position came up in Melbourne and I thought I might get it, but I didn't. Then an Australian agent found a potential position in Canberra, the country's capital. I flew to Sydney. Next day, my sister and I cheerfully drove the three or so hours to Canberra. She waited in the car park.

'You're as white as a sheet,' she said when I returned.

'He told me it had taken him 25 years to get into this country and that I would never get in. Then he threw my CV on the floor, just missing the bin.'

'What! What did you say?'

'Nothing, I just retrieved it and left.'

I think I was shaking. The agent, who had been present, was pretty taken aback too. The problem was that in peaceful Australia, my CV looked fanciful. I expect that, like others, he just couldn't believe the extent of my experience in trauma surgery. How could there be 100 to 150 trauma patients at one hospital in a 24-hour period unless it was in a warzone? He probably thought I was making it up.

There was some basis to this thinking. For instance, I claimed I had been involved in and had presented on more than a dozen repairs of a particularly rare condition in the neck involving the jugular foramen. This is the small bony canal in the base of the skull through which the large jugular vein passes as it drains all the blood from the brain. Several very important but delicate cranial nerves pass through this canal too and can be damaged during trauma, as happened with that policeman who was shot on duty.

While these nerves can also be damaged by a tumour, traumatic damage is extremely rare and hardly seen in Australia. In my CV, I just stated how many I had been involved in without substantiating the claim. While I had formally presented these cases to colleagues after the fact, I had never written them up and published them. In that phase of my career, demands were so high that we never stopped to think, 'Ah, this might be worth trying to publish.' We just moved on to the next patient. Also, senior surgeons were way too busy to mentor us in the art of publishing or to build a culture of research. We just rotated around the coalface and as a result, I had no hard proof.

That night, we booked into a Canberra hotel that had black-painted corridors, rooms and bathrooms. The black mirrored my mood. I spent a jetlagged night alone, not knowing where I was. But as usual, sunlight brought relief and the next morning I was okay. Meanwhile we had heard of a possibility in Perth, said to be the most isolated major city in the world. Many South Africans go to Perth because it feels similar to home, and although the landscape looked entirely unfamiliar, as soon as I landed I had a sense that this would be the place. So, I called Linda and told her.

'Have you had your interview?' she asked.

'No, I've just walked into the airport terminal.'

'For God's sake, just drop the intuition! I'm never going to Perth.' She was furious. 'If we absolutely have to go, then go back to Sydney or Melbourne and get a job there.'

In Perth, the two days of interviews began with my sitting in a circle with all the ENT consultants and telling them about myself. Then I was shown around the hospital and taken for dinner. They were all very hospitable and friendly. It appeared to go well but nothing further was said, although they promised to let me know if I had been successful. I could see what needed to be done with the hospital's ENT department, and on the flight home I drew up a plan to improve it.

At home a week passed, then another. I was getting nervous. After the fourth week I wrote to them, asking if there was any progress and attached my plan. They called back. 'We really liked you, but unfortunately the job will be going to an Australian.' When I reported this to Linda, she had a lot to say regarding my intuition. I slumped.

A month or so later, out of the blue, an offer came. The hospital couldn't get an Australian ENT to work full-time in the government health sector because the money wasn't good enough and so much more could be made in the private sector. Would I be interested in a six-month contract on a temporary visa during which I would only be allowed to work under supervision? My family and I would be entitled to no government benefits, such as Medicare. The job would begin in eight weeks, on Tuesday 27 January 2009. While the date aligned perfectly with my private pledge at the edge of the soccer field, it seemed odd to be starting a new job on a Tuesday, at the end of the month.

The administrative person on the phone said the other condition was that I accept or decline in 24 hours. I told her I had already made the decision. She was surprised and said I'd be crazy to accept these conditions. I didn't hesitate and, after a brief discussion with Linda, who hated the idea, I formally accepted the offer. This wasn't a foot in the door, it was toenail – but it was all I had.

Then we started telling our friends. They were gobsmacked that it was actually going ahead. I put on a strong front and hardened to all objections and arguments, and the subtle process of excommunication that had begun months before escalated. People were sort of closing me out, and in return I sort of closed them out. It was the only way forward: I didn't have the mental strength to accommodate their judgement, to calm the nervousness our move engendered in them, or to assuage the guilt I genuinely felt at leaving. The talk was all about how I was tearing Linda and the children away – and that was my talk too. I was full of justifications about security and the safety of the family. What I wasn't facing was that I was also tearing myself away. I obliterated that with tasks.

First, I had to find someone suitable to take over my practice, a person well qualified who would genuinely care for my patients. I found someone and all but handed it over. Under Shamim's ongoing careful supervision, this man would look after Madiba's hearing too – if Madiba agreed. As everyone knew we were in a rush, we had no leverage and our immovable assets were destined to go cheap. So we held a fire sale. Our cars went well below cost and we took the first undervalued offer on our house. The serious diminishment of our material wealth was one thing; the gradual erosion of friendships, community connections and professional relationships was another, and it hurt differently. Linda worked harder than I did and was much better at maintaining her connections.

Only my mother, who lived alone and was no longer strong, gave us a full, heartfelt blessing to leave. In a sense, she had the most to lose through our migration. We lived nearby, we popped in and out; she often spent Friday nights with us, she saw the children a lot during school holidays and occasionally she came away with us. With migration, that whole dimension would be lost to her, and us. She had long ago said farewell to my two sisters, and her belief that it was right for us to go was unwavering. 'I'll bless the day you land in Australia. It's best for the children, and you and Linda will find your way,' she said. 'Over time, you won't regret this. It will turn out well.'

While some people manage the process of leaving intelligently by keeping a foothold in South Africa while establishing a new base abroad, we didn't think of that, nor did we have the time to plan it. To the casual observer, it looked like yet another couple of well-to-do doctors abandoning a country that could barely afford to lose them. By comparison, there was a wealth of talent in Australia and our arrival on that continent would be entirely irrelevant. I was putting the selfish needs of my family ahead of everything else. There was nothing more to it.

For the next task, I would need all my courage. I would have to tell Madiba – who had always put the struggle ahead of his family – I was planning to leave for the sake of my family. I didn't know how this would unfold, and I tossed and turned for a couple of nights before our next appointment.

CHAPTER 27

The silent promise

WITH DREAD IN MY HEART, I drove to the Nelson Mandela Foundation offices down the road from Madiba's house. It was late 2008 and for the past nine years, I'd always driven this route with pleasurable anticipation. But now, about ten months after the murder of my school friend and five months after Madiba's birthday celebration, I was on my way to tell him I was leaving and abandoning South Africa. I knew this was going to be my most difficult meeting with him ever.

I pulled over to steady myself. Madiba had given his life for the struggle, he'd missed seeing his children grow up, he'd missed building a life with Winnie and he'd missed the warm tumble of family that I had taken for granted. Here I was, a white person born into opportunity, about to turn away from the country that had provided it.

I opened the car windows and pushed my seat back.

When I closed my eyes, as had happened so often before, I saw my friend's young sons coming off the soccer field, disbelieving at first, then distraught. As with so many traumatic events I had witnessed, I could still smell the scene. Then I thought of my children. I started the engine. To lighten my discomfort, I told myself that maybe Linda and I, or some of our children, would return some day.

Although I knew Madiba was uniquely forgiving and not judgemental, as the gate opened and I drove into the grounds of the Foundation, I was terrified. That this meeting was not at his home made it slightly easier. As usual, our sessions were closed and we had privacy. That was a wonderful thing about our meetings: we were always in our own bubble.

We went through the usual formalities and I settled into my work. I removed his hearing aids, cleaned them and examined his ears. I quickly ran out of medical things to do and could defer no longer. I had thought about how to frame my news and had rehearsed it, but in the moment I couldn't bring it to mind. So, I launched:

'Madiba, I would like to explain, as I've told you prior to this, that I will be leaving South Africa. I'm desperately worried about the criminal situation and I want my children to experience life without it.

'Although I've accepted a job in Australia which would require me to leave in a few weeks, I have come to tell you, to ask your opinion and, although this order of events is unorthodox, to ask for your permission, retrospectively, to go.'

He was sitting very still, almost stern, and looking at me intently. I continued.

'I have also come to thank you for the honour of being

allowed to treat you. For me, this time has been very mean-ingful, and I am going to miss you. I would like to ask your permission to come and visit you when I return to South Africa in the future.'

I fell silent, not knowing what to expect.

Madiba stared at me without expression for what seemed like an eternity, and I felt ashamed. Then, in that deep and deliberate voice that I'd come to know so well, he said, 'No, doctor ...' and after a long pause, 'don't think that you are so clever.'

I could feel shock course through my body. *Oh God, here it comes. He's going to tell me don't be a bloody coward, don't run away, don't be so clever.*

Then he repeated himself. 'No, doctor, don't think you are so clever. I went to Australia many, many years before you.'

What did he mean? I was puzzled. Was he telling me not to go? Then he explained. When he had been in prison, even though Madiba and his fellow inmates were allowed newspapers towards the end of their term, intelligence was smuggled in and out. They learned that a mass movement to end apartheid was underway, and this gave them heart. They knew about rallies held by the Free Nelson Mandela movement, which had originated in the UK. They also knew that a second movement had grown in Australia. Madiba said he got word out that when he was released from prison – he always believed he would be – among the first places he would visit outside of Africa would be the UK and Australia.

As he hadn't had the luxury of looking at an atlas or map for three decades – he was underground for three years before he was arrested – he told me he was only vaguely aware of where Australia was. But he was true to his word. His first visit beyond the African continent was to the UK. Then in October 1990, after a stop in Asia, he flew to Australia.

This was such a crucial juncture for me that his words seared themselves into my memory:

'Doctor, that was the longest trip of my life. I sat on this aeroplane and I thought we would never get to Australia. It must have been at the end of the world because we flew, and we flew, and we flew. When we arrived in Canberra, we had a big state dinner with lots of dignitaries, Prime Minister Bob Hawke and many, many others.

'During dinner, one of my assistants came to me and told me that there was a very important call that I needed to take. So, I went to the telephone. On the telephone, there was an Aboriginal leader who was very upset with me. He was shouting at me and said, "How dare you come to Australia. You are the leader of all the oppressed peoples in the world. And you are sitting at a white man's table. And you have ignored the Indigenous people of this country. You have not asked us for permission to come onto Country. You have not asked us to sit at your table."

'Doctor, I wasn't fully aware of the history of Australia. I'd been in prison for 27 years and I had not studied anything about the Aboriginal people and their persecution. I apologised to this man, but he said it was too late and my apology was not good enough. I needed to visit with the elders and receive a "Welcome to Country" ceremony. I apologised again and that was the end of the conversation.

'I came back to the table, and I was upset. When I sat down, those around asked what had happened. I relayed the story to them and one of the great leaders at the table went like this with his hand [Madiba brushed his hand away]. "Oh, don't worry, we'll sort it out," he said. Doctor, only when I saw this white man's gesture did I fully realise the importance of that phone call and the very serious mistake I had made. I understood the Aboriginal people's suffering and the fact that this had been ignored not only by the people at the table but by me.'

'So, what did you do?'

'I immediately called my assistant to the table and asked for a meeting the following day, with the Indigenous leader or leaders, even if it meant cancelling something else. We were due to go to Sydney or Melbourne the next day and I was determined to have this meeting, and if necessary, a plane should be arranged for 7 o'clock in the morning.'

Madiba said an unofficial meeting was arranged and, against protocol, he slipped away for it, without his security detail or entourage.

'And so, doctor, I want to tell you, don't think you are so clever, because I thought I was so clever. I was arrogant. Never use ignorance as an excuse as I did. Make sure you thoroughly study the places you are going to, the history and all its peoples.

'And doctor, wherever you go in the world, read about the Indigenous people, and give them the respect that I failed to give in Australia. There is no excuse.

'We are all part of humanity. If you go anywhere in the world and you contribute to the underprivileged, it doesn't matter if it is in Africa or Australia or for that matter anywhere else. If you do that you have my permission.'

When I heard that I cried, openly and unashamedly.

CHAPTER 28

The leaving

WHAT HAD JUST happened? As I drove away, I turned it over and over in my mind. Perhaps I had misunderstood? I never knew he had been to Australia almost 20 years earlier. Back at my desk, I checked it out. The evidence was there in print and on video, and I began to appreciate the depth of his mistake. I also gave myself a much-needed crash course in colonialism in Australia.

A meeting with Aboriginal representatives had indeed been put on his official run sheet for Sydney, later in the itinerary, but Indigenous activists were so upset by his failure to request their permission to come to the land that they called for a boycott. The act of asking for permission would have acknowledged them as the traditional owners and custodians of the land, which they had been for more than 60 000 years. A ritual welcoming ceremony would have been staged, ensuring mutual respect and understanding between visitor and host.

When Madiba arrived at Parliament House in Canberra, Aboriginal activist Michael Mansell staged a conspicuous one-man protest. He waved an Aboriginal flag and shouted, 'What about Aborigines, Mr Mandela? Why doesn't someone say something about the Aboriginal people in this country?'

Madiba was apparently ignorant of the fact that the British had massacred whole populations in a coordinated attempt to 'breed out' Aboriginal people. He also didn't know that First Nations people carry the burden of this intergenerational trauma and were still fighting for their voices to be heard. Unaware, Madiba went on to give a long speech thanking Australia for its anti-apartheid activism, its sports boycotts and its financial help. He made no mention of the plight of the Indigenous people.

The embarrassing irony came a little later, when he was asked why he hadn't raised the issue of the way Aboriginal people were treated. He explained that he didn't want to 'interfere' in the internal politics of another country. What?! So many other nations had done all they could to interfere in apartheid, and Madiba had honoured and remained loyal to them. He didn't know that Aboriginal people had come out strongly against apartheid too.

The message for me was that every country has an indigenous history that needs to be acknowledged, studied and understood. There is no excuse for ignorance. It was significant that 19 years after that excruciating event, he was telling me this. It must have been hard-wired in him. No wonder he was warning me. He'd made a political, diplomatic and humanitarian blunder. When he returned to Australia a decade later, in September 2000, he made good. While his original sin was largely forgiven, it was not forgotten. Activists said he'd missed a golden opportunity to draw world attention to the circumstances of an oppressed people who are among the oldest living cultures on earth.

This was not a request for a grand gesture or for the Australian government to be humiliated, just for the Aboriginal people to be recognised. They pointed to a visit by Muhammad Ali in 1979. During that visit he had diverted from his schedule and spent three unscripted hours in an Aboriginal health service in Melbourne. On the ground, word spread and waves of people rolled in. It became a landmark event. At the time, he was the most famous black man on the planet. Eleven years later, Madiba was. And ten years after that, he still was.

Before he was elected president, Madiba stated that human rights would be the light that would guide his government's foreign policy. The country fell in behind this ideal, and under his guardianship, it is widely agreed that South Africa temporarily earned international prestige.

I saw Madiba one last time, and he took care to remind me of my obligation.

I once heard that conflict can make separation easier. It was in an article about men who worked on oil rigs, two weeks on and two weeks off. It showed that just before they left home, yet again, the relationship with their partners often deteriorated. The anticipation of their departure created tension and made things scratchy. There was a sense in the household that they should 'just go already'. In a diluted way, I got that feeling from our community.

When the removal vans arrived at our house, I couldn't look. When they had gone, Linda locked herself in our empty bedroom, lay on the bare Oregon pine floor and wept. We went through our own rituals of leaving. To water down my anxiety, I thought of my grandparents fleeing their small villages in central Europe without the possibility of ever returning. We would only be a nine-hour flight away. Then came the farewells. There was no party, just a series of visits. Most of our friends preferred to talk about other things.

Saying goodbye to Rachel Hiine and Lizzie Machosa, the two women who had dedicated years to serving our family, was distressing and complicated. They had played an important role in bringing up our children while some of their own children were brought up by their relatives in their rural homes. Our children wept as they hugged them goodbye. The least we could do was to use some of the proceeds from the sale of our house towards the building of modest houses for them.

Our eldest son was 21 years old, a student at Wits University and passionate about the future of South Africa. He was adamant about staying and announced his engagement to his girlfriend weeks before we left. We were sending our twin daughters on a post-school study trip overseas. This meant, at least initially, we would only have our two younger boys with us.

The time came to part from my mother. We stood in her small but beautiful garden, her refuge, without words.

Privately, she had coped with much pain in her life. Her mother had died when she was a child, our baby brother had been lost to a cot death and there'd been the long agony of our father's illness. She hugged me and repeated what she had said to both my sisters. 'I'm going to pretend to myself that you are just going away for a while.' Then she walked me to the gate and mouthed each letter in the words 'I love you'.

CHAPTER 29

Darwin and the Barnacle

A S OUR PLANE CLIMBED, I put my face to the window and watched the Hillbrow Tower and the mine dumps grow smaller. My head, still filled with the logistics of leaving, allowed no space for loss, but there was a dull tug in my heart. Yes, all the items on our lists had been crossed off, but so had my fidelity to the country that had nurtured me. I could feel as sentimental as I liked, and although I had made a contribution, the reality was that I was leaving the place that needed my skills. At the age of 47, I should not expect to have a career again. That, too, was over. Australia had no interest in my particular skill set.

On 20 January 2009, we arrived in a heatwave, hired a small car and went to the two-bedroom flat we'd rented online. I stayed with the kids while Linda went out to buy food. Then I went out to buy fans. She had cousins in Perth who embraced us and generously included us in their Australia

Day celebrations on the banks of Perth's Swan River.

As our first public outing, it was a flabbergasting experience. When multiple firecrackers went off, Linda and I and the children dived for cover. We thought they were gunshots. People laughed. I also couldn't understand how everyone was sitting on the foreshore with all their possessions – food, mobile phones, bags, blankets and chairs – laid out in front of them. And without a care in the world, they casually walked to and from their cars.

The next day, I started work at the Sir Charles Gairdner Hospital in Perth, on Whadjuk Country, the traditional lands of the Noongar people. It was one day short of 28 January, the date when my school friend had been shot. I always pause on that day, to remember him and that fateful night when something in me snapped.

In the first weeks, I stumbled around trying to understand the local idiom. The streetscapes were unfamiliar, the quality of the light was different and even the grass seemed a different colour. At the hospital, I hit one administrative hurdle after another. The standard of Australian public health care is world class and there is a genuine ethos of what the locals call 'a fair go', but to get it, you have to be in the system.

Medicine runs on acronyms but Australian hospitals take the use of them, and abbreviations and diminutives, to a new level. I started keeping a notebook and every time there was something I didn't understand, I wrote it down, asked for an explanation or looked it up. I was missing the nuances and was anxious about doing the wrong thing. I'd worked at St Mary's in London and had adapted much more easily to that hospital. What impressed me, however, was that the Australian system was very organised once you got to know it.

As it happened, the state's health service was recruiting ENT surgeons to fly to distant Aboriginal communities at fixed times during the year. My hand went up and I started going to the Kimberley, in far northern Western Australia. One of my first trips was to Kununurra, the remotest place I've ever been. During that two-week stint, I was desperately lonely in my bare room, missing my family. Nothing could be seen for miles, and to get phone reception I had to climb a hill. As I couldn't do that alone in the dark, the nights were long and solitary.

Once I had stopped fretting about what my life had come to, my mind began to roam beyond the selfish boundaries of my existence. I thought a lot about Madiba, how he had given up his family for the struggle and how I'd done exactly the opposite. How he had been in his mid to late forties when he was given a life sentence and how I was roughly the same age, beginning a new life in a new country. Although a grandiose comparison, it gave me comfort.

While Australia prides itself on its cultural diversity – and it is highly multicultural – it takes time to be accepted. People were naturally a little suspicious of me and, even now, some 15 years later, I'm still regarded as an immigrant. As a doctor, I'm still classified as an 'international medical graduate', or IMG. I remember going to a talk on inclusion in medicine by a female IMG who said, 'Australians think multiculturalism is inviting people to the party, but it's a long time before they ask you to dance!'

At one academic dinner for all ENTs in Perth, a prominent member of this specialist community recommended

I read the book *Darwin and the Barnacle*, and only then would he talk to me about medicine in Australia. So, I ordered the book and read it. It was the story of one tiny creature and history's most spectacular scientific breakthrough, and when I next bumped into him, he asked, 'Well, did you read it?'

'Yes.'

'Tell me, once Darwin had conceptualised and written *On the Origin of Species*, how long did it take before he decided to publish it?

'He waited eight years, because he thought they weren't ready for it.'

'Correct. And that's what you need to do. You need to wait eight years before people will have regard for you and take you seriously in Australia.'

Then I knew what I was up against. My strength is that people usually underestimate me, which, of course, provides an inherent advantage. While I won't disappoint them, I may exceed their expectations. That esteemed specialist wouldn't have been pleased to know just how much of a tonic this little exchange provided. It boosted my confidence. I was going to force myself onto the dance floor.

Meantime, Linda was struggling to adjust to Perth and aching to go home and rekindle her life and career. She was desperately unhappy. Our two boys were also lost: they had new school uniforms but no new friends yet. I was, however, more optimistic about their settling in.

When I'd arrived, the university had made me an adjunct (unpaid) junior lecturer and I'd been grateful for it. But when my six-month hospital contract was coming to an end, I learned that it would not be extended unless I had an academic position that was not an 'adjunct'. I had to drop that part of the title. The administrative secretary of the surgery department said I would have to reapply, and expressed some pessimism about my credentials.

By then, I had presented at an Australian conference and was actively involved in the hospital. I was also the only person teaching ENT to medical students and just beginning to get a tiny bit of recognition for it. Although I was officially teaching students from the University of Western Australia, when I saw students from the University of Notre Dame Australia walking aimlessly around the hospital, I started teaching them too. Some colleagues scratched their heads. Why, they asked, would I bother with them, given I was not being paid? The secretary was firm:

'You are going to have to submit a CV,' she said.

'I already did, when I emigrated.'

'Dr Friedland, we didn't read your CV.'

'I beg your pardon.'

'The university requires a specific format for a CV, and you need to comply with all its specifications, from font size to spacing, etcetera. Unless you do that, it won't be processed and it won't be read.'

'Are you joking?'

She glared at me for what felt like minutes. In that moment I learned my most valuable lesson about Australian bureaucracy. There is only one way. I said I'd get it done properly, and then she added, 'By the way, don't include your South African experience. It's not that relevant and we're not interested in it. And don't put your photograph in either.'

That left me with about five months of local experience. I paid a professional Australian editor to have the document perfectly checked and formatted, and at the end of the CV, submitted my South African experience anyway.

We were on tenterhooks. If I didn't get the position, our visas required us to leave the country before 27 July. Bali was the closest place to wait out fate and we booked tickets. The day before we were due to fly, I got a call.

'Congratulations, Professor Friedland, we've appointed you to an associate professorship,' the voice said.

'I'm afraid you've made a mistake; I was applying for a junior lectureship,' I replied.

'Yes, but after reviewing your CV we've given you the equivalence of a professor.'

I think I dropped my phone. I was in the system, and here was that famous 'fair go'.

Australia is a country of patience and process. Nothing happens in a hurry. I kept on hearing the phrase 'She'll be right, mate' and never understood what it meant. Things take time. In South Africa there was a constant sense of urgency and we lived on our nerves. This was the other side of the coin.

CHAPTER 30

Humble pies

ONE OF THE MIRACLES of Perth is that the cost of regular suburban houses is considerably lower than those in the southeast corner of Australia. So, we mortgaged ourselves to the maximum, got a house and then lived on a tight budget. After more than a year had passed, I returned alone to Johannesburg for a family event. After I'd covered the cost, I took a photograph of my bank statement. I had 23 cents in my account. But Linda and I still had South African credit cards and there were times when we survived by rotating them.

Although my university title was elevated, I was still low in the hospital hierarchy and was only allowed three days of leave, plus the weekend. I stayed with my mother and when I ventured beyond the bounds of our family, I felt like I was in no-man's land: I was not established in Australia, I was not financially secure, I was not at peace, and I was not sure I'd

done the right thing. People in Johannesburg weren't exactly
pushing to associate with me. They were busy, I wasn't part
of their lives any more, and they certainly didn't want to
talk about emigration. In the past, I'd seen people return
and crow about their successes abroad. If asked, I would
have talked about the complexities of such a drastic move.

Everyone I met in Johannesburg was flushed with World
Cup fever, full of anticipation, had secured good seats and
could talk of nothing else. As a football fan I would have sold
my shirt to be at any one of the games. I well remembered
the time in 2004 when South Africa had won the bid to host
the 2010 FIFA World Cup. Most particularly, I remembered
Madiba's cameo role in the bidding campaign, those refer-
ences to his playing football on Robben Island and how the
game made the prisoners feel alive and triumphant. Then
there were the photos of him lifting the legendary trophy.
During my visit, I knew he was not that well and very much
wanted to see him, but it was not possible. Those days of
easy access were gone.

Back in Perth I watched the opening ceremony, expecting
him to be there and, as usual, for the camera to seek him out
and dwell on him. But he wasn't. His great-granddaughter
had died in a car crash just before, so he had withdrawn and
was in mourning. Four weeks later, I found myself wondering
if he would be at the closing ceremony. The final was between
Spain and the Netherlands, and before it began, there was a
press report that FIFA had put 'extreme pressure' on Madiba
to attend.

His grandson, Mandla Mandela, spoke to a journalist
about the pressure and noted that FIFA did not seem to
understand the family's traditions and customs. He thought

it best for them to be left to grieve. But Madiba did turn up and thrilled the crowds by touring the field in a golf cart. I looked closely. He was a few days short of his ninety-second birthday and frail. That would be his final public appearance.

It had taken me a long time to absorb the lessons I received in that calm house where the temperature, the order in the rooms and Madiba in his chair seemed always to be the same. This memory is built into me and sometimes, in Australia, I revisit it. I'm waved through the gates and walk up to the house where the man who represented all our hopes is safely ensconced.

There is so much more I could have learned from him. He was a master of self-control. I could feel it when I was with him, but once outside his walls, I was too busy and distracted to slow down and think about this. Only in Australia, when I hit dire straits, was I determined to rein in my impulsivity.

Although a bit shaky when I arrived in Perth, I was used to being top of the heap, and those around me had no difficulty recognising my 'sense of authority', a character flaw they would say is common in white South African expats. The theory goes that apartheid gave us an inflated sense of our worth, a distaste for self-criticism and the belief that we are right and will succeed. I am guilty as charged and, in my third year in Australia, it led to an outburst which even today I much regret.

It was an 'off day' in theatre. The nursing staff was distracted, the case before me had unusual complications and everything took twice as long to complete. I was at the edge of my tolerance, but thankfully the operation was successful. I can't explain it, but the next morning when

I arrived at that theatre, I had a brain attack. Without provocation, I roundly berated everyone, from the nurses to the technicians, to the CEO of the hospital himself, announcing from on high that I had absolutely no faith in him or his hospital. Before the last offensive comment left my mouth, I knew I'd gone too far.

It wasn't long before I was called in by the CEO, who had his executive and legal teams in his office with, I expected, a resolution to dismiss me. I apologised profusely and was sincerely and most deeply sorry. I said I didn't know what came over me and would do everything in my power to develop some self-mastery to ensure that such an outburst would not occur again. To his credit, the CEO accepted my undertaking and gave me some humiliating homework. I had to meet with the nurses and other staff, I had to apologise to each one and had to write a series of letters. Much humble pie had to be eaten.

After that, professionally, things got progressively better and I was able to build a reasonable career at the hospital, with a research component, a private practice and some work with Indigenous communities. As a family, we went back to South Africa a few more times and the social awkwardness disappeared. The Covid-19 pandemic grounded us and when, after a five-year break, we visited again, I was in for a shock.

CHAPTER 31

Overdreaming

WHEN WE TOUCHED DOWN in Johannesburg in November 2022, the airport was well lit and seemed completely functional. We picked up a hire car but soon found ourselves driving into darkness. The state was in the grip of a power shortage and 'load shedding' meant large sections of the city had no house, street or traffic lights. Creeping through familiar but darkened suburbs was nerve-wracking, but not unexpected. We knew South Africa was in deep trouble and that the energy crisis was just one manifestation. Rates of poverty, unemployment, corruption and crime were soaring. But there was something we didn't know and would never have expected.

We'd been advised to book accommodation with a generator, and suddenly our hotel came into view on a small hill, shining like a beacon. It was safe and comfortable. Whenever there was a shift between the grid and the generator, a micro blackout would ripple through our rooms. It was only a moment long, but it reminded us of where we were. I told my children that when I grew up, a couple of kilometres north of this hotel, I never gave electricity a thought. Like the sky, it was always there. Back then, I also never gave a thought to most of the South African children my age who lived without electricity and, if they were fortunate enough to be going to school, would have been doing their homework by candlelight. Now, half a century later, candles were as useful as ever.

The next morning, I had a mission. It was to drive the usual route to the corner plot in Houghton, where Madiba's house stood. I hoped to recapture that feeling of warm anticipation, to walk around the walls and to see how things were. But it was no place for nostalgia. The house was almost derelict, wires from the vandalised security system swung free, paint was peeling and the roof needed repair. The pavement garden that had been so carefully tended was now unloved and overgrown. In Madiba's last months, well-wishers had painted messages of hope and admiration on stones and arranged them in flower beds on the manicured pavement. Although some of the lettering was fading, the stones were still there between the weeds.

Next, I drove a few blocks down the road to the Nelson Mandela Foundation. I was the only visitor that morning and found my way to his office, which was kept just as it had been when he had last used it. It was possible to take a few steps into the room. I did and as I looked around, I remembered it all. This was a place for nostalgia and I revisited it twice more that trip. I also bought all the books on display that I didn't already have.

I returned to the Wits Donald Gordon Medical Centre, where I met with Shamim, Angie and Petronella, an administrative assistant who used to run my hearing clinic. We had an intimate lunch, reminiscing about Madiba and our experiences. Then Petronella and Shamim bravely broached the subject of my unpleasant behaviour in the months leading up to my departure and described how it had affected them and others. During those months, friends, colleagues and staff had persisted in trying to persuade me to change my decision. I had been tense. I had been abrupt. I had been rude. Although I felt ghastly about this and was ashamed, I was grateful Petronella and Shamim had revealed my blind side. I apologised and we all hugged.

My family had always encouraged me to document my experiences with Madiba. They said I'd had a unique privilege and that I should share some of my insights. As I approached my sixtieth birthday, my sister Jill, who lives in Sydney, generously offered me a gift. She would help me write this book. Jill is a biographer and a leading medical journalist in Australia. We have always been close and, through writing and researching this book, we relived the experience together. At times it was gruelling as Jill pushed me to go deeper, forcing me to articulate very complex feelings and concepts. We spent uncountable hours together in Perth, Sydney and South Africa. Between our busy schedules, we were on Zoom and email and spoke endlessly on the phone at crazy hours. We laughed, we cried, we got exasperated and we found new sources of energy. Occasionally Linda joined us, and all the children were interested. During our trip to South Africa, friends met us for dinner at the hotel and when I mentioned I was writing a book that involved Madiba, they were not impressed. They looked at me blankly or shrugged, as if to say, 'Why would you want to do that?' When I'd heard similar sentiments three or four times, I realised a change was underway. One public intellectual whom I admired waved her hand and said, 'Oh God, no one will read it. Don't bother.'

Confused and rather upset, I began to read whatever I could, and the picture became clearer. Outside South Africa people spoke Mandela's name with reverence; inside the country his legacy was being revised – not by everyone, but by enough people to be noticed. I don't want to overstate this – statues of him were not being toppled, and he was not being trashed – but his reputation was being tarnished. I hadn't noticed any of this on my previous visit, in 2017, but was told it had already been stirring then. What was driving it?

People were quite open on the subject. Although Madiba had saved the country from violent revolution, the ideal future he had imagined for the new rainbow nation had not eventuated. It had fallen terribly short, leaving millions of people poor, hungry, disillusioned and disappointed. With no one else to blame, many sheeted the responsibility back to him. He was the first black president; why hadn't he put a better template in place, one that would hold for the future?

I've heard it suggested that disillusionment with Madiba was probably what De Klerk hoped for when he released him in 1990. Back then, Madiba was perceived as having mythical powers, a man capable of miracles, and the theory went that once he was released people would see he was human. By putting him through his political paces, they would see he could make mistakes too. De Klerk was a far-sighted man, and likely expected that the myth would eventually evaporate, leaving only a man. Who could have known that this revision would take 25 to 30 years?

When I questioned my black colleagues about the tarnish, some felt Madiba had overcompromised and left the white population with too many of its ill-gotten gains. It was never a fair arrangement. Although there had been housing, water and electricity provision for some of the country's most disadvantaged, it was negligible given the need and the scale of the inequity. Just look, they said, how the gap had grown. They had little sympathy for the counter-view that the solution might have taken generations.

Some of my white liberal colleagues were no kinder. They said Madiba had had the unique opportunity to build a new governance structure from scratch, one that was imbued with a culture that would not tolerate the corruption and the state capture that was now destroying the government. They said this failing had been exacerbated by a transition that had taken place too rapidly. People without experience had been parachuted into top jobs in administration, the public service, industry, mining and just about every other important activity. They may have been educated and intelligent, but they needed more time to build a knowledge base and develop the appropriate expertise.

No one suggested Madiba had been corrupt. They acknowledged that he'd been full of noble ideals, which he'd kept alive. But with no machinery to carry them forward, they had fizzled out. Young graduates, who had been urged to pursue tertiary education, couldn't find work. For them, reality had killed any remaining hope and there was no trace of the excitement of the Mandela dream. Mandela had overpromised and perhaps desperate South Africans had overdreamed. There were many other theories too. Some said he was a statesman, not a politician, into the big picture and not into bureaucracy. Some said he paid too much attention to international matters and not enough to domestic ones. And so the discontent went.

While it looked like the man who had helped the country avoid a bloody revolution had become the scapegoat for its troubled transition into the new world, I thought about it differently. It seemed to me that we were witnessing a phase in the heroic cycle, and that with time, as South Africa stabilised, disappointment would dissipate and the cycle would turn. Were the country to flourish, he would again become a universal hero. To me, Madiba was a healer who restored relationships not just between nations but between races, cultures and creeds. He was probably the most inspirational figure of the late twentieth century and there is no question that he will keep his place in world history.

Madiba's final couple of years were very difficult as he battled various disabilities, including heart and breathing problems, and was in and out of hospital, sometimes for long periods. He had fully retreated from the public eye. On a few occasions he told me he felt tired and was ready to go to his ancestors. He reiterated a number of times that he did not want to linger. When I heard he had been in hospital for several months, I knew this was not what he had wanted.

My twin brother, Richard, helped where he could. As it happened, our mother, Selma, had also been ill towards the end of her life. After an operation, she was unhappy in hospital, so Richard persuaded her to recuperate in his house. For her comfort and to make nursing easier, he went out and bought a high-tech ICU bed. When she no longer needed it, he paid it forward. Others used it and, when Madiba needed such a bed in his last months at home in Houghton, Richard had it delivered.

Madiba died at that home in December 2013 and was buried in Qunu.

CHAPTER 32

Background noise

THE LAST TIME I saw Madiba, I was 47. At home
that night, after the visit, I found myself dwelling
on my own vulnerabilities. My siblings and I had
grown up in the shadow of our father's illness and we
watched ourselves for symptoms like his. That was a given.

But recently, a suspicion had been growing in me that
I too might have hearing loss. Over the next few years, I had
myself assessed intermittently and was always told my
hearing was more or less normal for my age.

Then it changed. In 2018, I was recruited as an ENT
surgeon for the Royal Australian Air Force. I was to serve as
a specialist reservist for an expeditionary health squadron
tasked with providing medical assistance in local and international disaster relief and humanitarian aid missions.

Before admission, they put me through a rigorous bat-
tery of health checks, which included a detailed hearing

assessment. The results left me astonished. I had significant noise-induced hearing loss in the high frequencies. While some of it was age-related, the audiograms produced a pattern typical of occupational noise exposure. There was only one place that was coming from – the operating theatre.

And it wasn't only from the machines that beep at high frequency or the noise of the high-pressure suction devices; it was from the high-speed ear drills. When I use them for cochlear or mastoid operations, it is always in close proximity to my own ears. While we wear a lot of protective gear in theatre, we can't afford the luxury of wearing earplugs too. They might muffle or mute crucial exchanges between the theatre team.

The Air Force results woke me up. When there was background noise, I was indeed struggling to hear what people were saying. The Air Force required me to have a brain scan and an evaluation by an independent hearing specialist. The scan was clear, and while the specialist was equivocal about whether I should wear hearing aids, on balance she thought them unnecessary. 'Why wear them?' she asked. 'Why be seen to be wearing them? Think of what your colleagues may think.'

Although more than a decade had passed since I last saw Madiba, the example he'd set was seared into me. He didn't care about the stigma; he cared about improving function. Appearances didn't matter to him; reality did.

If there was a chance they could help, I would wear them and do so without regard to stigma. So, I went ahead and purchased a pair of in-the-ear-canal aids, the kind I had originally recommended for Madiba.

I regard myself to be in a transition phase where I use

my hearing aids intermittently, at select occasions such as meetings and conferences. They are not perfect, and they irritate me, but they help enormously. It took about eight weeks to get used to them and for my brain to adapt to the fact that they also magnify sounds I don't want to hear. For me, they are useless in noisy restaurants or at loud concerts.

During the pandemic, they were helpful during ward rounds, when everyone was wearing a mask and speech was indistinct. I could hear what patients were saying. But I couldn't wear them in the operating theatre because they magnify sound.

I'm always thinking about ear protection, and on a commercial plane I take noise-cancelling earphones, regardless of the length of the flight. In the Air Force, everyone uses hearing protection; in fact, the pilots wear double ear protection. And I do too. I continue to have hearing assessments.

My family is largely unaware of how or when I use my hearing aids and the few people I've alerted to my hearing loss still speak softly and make no allowances for it. I have tried to educate colleagues, from dentists to orthopaedic surgeons, about the risks of using medical drills, but they just shrug, either in denial or resignation.

I persist, because there is no benefit in delaying using hearing assistance when it's needed. The literature shows that men are reluctant to admit hearing loss and usually delay getting help for seven to ten years, often unaware of the impact it is having at work and in their family.

Most importantly, I persevere because there is a clear link between hearing loss, mild cognitive impairment and cognitive loss. We are not sure of the extent to which this is due to the pathology of ageing of the ear, the ageing brain or their interaction. Researchers are trying to determine whether this is a top-down effect, meaning an ageing brain accelerates hearing loss, or if this is a bottom-up effect, where hearing loss reduces cognition, or a combination of both.

Either way, there is strong evidence that hearing sound and speech stimulates areas of the brain that are important in sustaining cognition. In 2020, the prestigious medical journal *The Lancet* found that 40 per cent of worldwide dementias are caused by 12 modifiable risk factors. The most prevalent was hearing loss. There is also evidence that treating hearing loss is important in improving executive function and memory in people with dementia. For me, these are good enough reasons to wear hearing aids.

Quite often, when I put my devices in, Madiba is with me. Although I think of him at other times too, I am no longer so nostalgic for all that I left behind. The peace of mind, the equanimity and the sense of security our family enjoy in Australia are priceless and I'm exceptionally grateful that we landed on these shores. My internal landscape will always be South African, but I have developed an affection for the Australian Outback and for the long, beautiful beaches of Western Australia, washed by the ocean they share with Africa.

Acknowledgements

Several people have helped us with this book, and we gladly acknowledge them. Thank you to my wife, Linda, an author of seven health books, who patiently read all iterations of the text, sustained my enthusiasm for the task and supported me. The dedication and editing skills of Jill's daughter, Sarah Margo, significantly improved this manuscript. The energy and persistence of Peter Kash, Florida, USA, together with his belief in the relevance of this project, boosted our sometimes flailing confidence.

Working with our excellent publisher, Sibongile Machika, was such a pleasure, and sincere thanks to her for her insight and guidance. Gratitude to Annie Olivier, Publishing Director, Jonathan Ball Publishers, and to Catriona Ross, who did the final edit, polishing and vastly improving this text.

My twin brother Richard played a crucial role, as did Sandra Vandermerwe. We received invaluable advice from Leonard Berelowitz, my sister Sally-Anne Friedland, Patricia

215

Jacobs, Peter Lilienfeld and Dunay Schmulian. My thanks also, to Emanuel Klein and Jane Singleton, Kate Baumwol, Siobhan Hey and Tony Hey. My enduring thanks go to my children, Gavriel, Leora, Yael, Aharon and Benjamin.

Although we read and drew on many books, documents and multimedia reports about Madiba, any mistakes are our own.

Peter Friedland,
Perth, March 2024

Sources

Listed below are some of the books and other materials used for background information for this book.

Barnard, Rita, *The Cambridge Companion to Nelson Mandela*, Cambridge University Press, 2014

Carlin, John, *Playing the Enemy: Nelson Mandela and the Game that Made a Nation*, Atlantic Books, 2008

Funde, Sonwabo Eddie, *Man on a Mission: 30 Years of Exile for the Freedom of his Nation*, Sifiso Publishers (second edition), 2019

Gregory, James, *Goodbye Bafana: Nelson Mandela, My Prisoner, My Friend*, Headline Book Publishing, 1995

Hatang, Sello and Harris, Verne, *I Know This To be True: Nelson Mandela: Guiding Principles*, Nelson Mandela Foundation in association with Blackwell & Ruth, 2020

Joffe, Joel and Block, David, private correspondence, 2009

Maharaj, Mac and Kathrada, Ahmed, *Mandela: The Authorised Portrait*, Five Mile Press in association with PQ Blackwell, 2006

Mandela, Ndaba, *11 Life Lessons from Nelson Mandela*, Penguin Random House UK, 2018

Mandela, Nelson, *The Illustrated Long Walk to Freedom*, Little, Brown and Company, 1996

Mandela, Nelson, *Nelson Mandela By Himself: The Authorised Book of Quotations*, Pan Macmillan South Africa, 2011

Mandela, Nelson and Langa, Mandla, *Dare Not Linger: The Presidential Years*, Pan Macmillan, 2017

Naidoo, Vimla and Venter, Sahm, *I Remember Nelson Mandela*, Jacana Media in association with Nelson Mandela Foundation, 2018

'Nelson Mandela's exemplary legacy for South Africa', Modern Diplomacy, 2023, available at https://moderndiplomacy.eu/2023/07/19/nelson-mandelas-exemplary-legacy-for-south-africa/ and accessed on 12 February 2024

Saks, David, *Jewish Memories of Mandela*, South African Jewish Board of Deputies, 2011

Smith, David James, *Young Mandela: The Revolutionary Years*, Weidenfeld & Nicolson, 2010

South African Jewish Board of Deputies, *Madiba: A Tribute from South African Jewry*, SAJBD, 2008

Steinberg, Jonny, *Winnie & Nelson: Portrait of a Marriage*, Knopf Publishing Group, 2023

About the authors

PROFESSOR PETER FRIEDLAND is a leading ear, nose and throat surgeon and holds the academic chair in this discipline in Western Australia. Most of his career was spent in South Africa, where he was clinical head of the department of ENT at the University of the Witwatersrand Donald Gordon Medical Centre.

JILL MARGO is a best-selling author specialising in biography, memoir and health. Her books have been translated into three languages, with one republished in India. She is also a multi-award-winning journalist on *The Australian Financial Review*.